PACKING
MY BAGS

PACKING MY BAGS

Two Sides to the Story of a Life with Horses

JULIE ULRICH

FOUR
IN HAND

PRESS

First published in 2024
by Four-In-Hand Press
an Imprint of Trafalgar Square Books
North Pomfret, Vermont 05053

ISBN: 978-1-64601-263-3
A Library of Congress Control Number is available on file.

Photos courtesy of the author unless otherwise noted.
Main cover photo by SAS Equestrian, Shawna Whitty, first printed in *Sidelines* magazine and used with permission.

Book cover and interior design by RM Didier
Typefaces: Adonis, Goldenbook
Printed in the United States of America
10 9 8 7 6 5 4 3 2 1

DEDICATION

To all who read the story
and find a happy life with horses

CONTENTS

INTRODUCTION

To introduce my book, I must introduce myself. In the very first case, let it be known that I'm a typical Gemini. As such, I have two sides to my personality. One side, the adventurous and imaginative side, got me into a lot of trouble (and a lot of fun) when I was young. The other side is intense, hardworking, and dedicated to tradition, which pushed me to my education and helped me in my training of both horses and riders. In this book, you will find both of these sides.

The chapters of my life story, and the travels and adventures that fell in my path, were fun to remember and easy to write. They describe, for the most part, the adventurous part of my life. Of course, this side of my life has been greatly fed by the era that I have lived. By recounting my personal history, I hope to describe the adventure and diversity that is open to all, in any era, who open their eyes to trying things.

The educational articles that are slipped in between chapters throughout the book represent the more serious side of my personality. These articles are arranged in this way so you do not become overwhelmed with theory. This side of my life and education in horses has given me what I hope to leave with my reader: an open door to the possibility of connection with an animal so magical as the horse.

There are references throughout the book to the various classical methods of equitation that I have studied. I spent a lot of time reading about them. I spent even more time riding to try to master the rudiments of the classics. I realize that this is not the way for many who ride in the present era. In an effort to encourage a return to the classical system of riding, I will mention some of them here to forewarn you. And, at the end of the book, I will include some of the easier, but correct, books with which an interested rider might begin.

The Caprilli method, originating in Italy, has been credited with the basic system for hunter riding. It encourages an open frame and self-carriage from the horse, and a forward seat and a light or non-existent contact with the rider's hands. In America, Chamberlain, Littauer, and Gordon Wright methods took many of Caprilli's ideas and were the path of evolution into the American System. The American System, involving forward, light riding using blood horses, has been considered the ideal in the world by many.

This system was affected enormously by Bert de Nemethy, who was brought to the United States by Eleanora Sears in the fifties and who practiced the Hungarian method. Bert was not the only top horseman using the Hungarian method. There were many others who also wrote about this method and practiced it. However, Bert was the most articulate. He was also patient, kind, and imaginative. His knowledge of gymnastic training for jumpers saved our lives at the beginning of his tenure, and Americans have never lost this education.

The closest system to the American system is the French system. Although there is a wonderful French system of dressage, with collection and all the movements of the Grand Prix, the jumping disciplines are all based on forward riding, long necks, and self-carriage. French riding is based on activity and lightness, and only a mature horse is asked to shorten. The French breeds of Anglo-Arab, AQPS (Other than Thoroughbred), and Selle Français are blood horses with an emphasis on the gallop. They suit the system and must explain the evolution of it.

The German system was only different by the importance given to collection and to the horse's acceptance of a firmer connection to the rein. The system was suited to the majority of the breeds found in the North. They were slightly heavier, with a better trot than canter, and a rider was more supportive with his aids than on the freer blood horse ridden in France. This system has evolved enormously in my lifetime to accommodate the modern German breeding program. It now approaches the lighter and freer riding of other countries.

The Weyrother Method was taught at the Spanish Riding School. It was one of several methods taught there and is an extremely clear and precise way of riding dressage. It is ideally suited for a Lipizzaner, but also for a confused or nervous horse. It is a wonderful foundation for a rider due to the precision in the use of the aids. The timing of the aids is a priority, and the classical sequences of training steps build an extremely calm horse and an extremely competent rider.

There are other schools of riding coming from Portugal, Sweden, and Poland. They were all practiced at the National School and suited the breed of the country. As the National schools closed, due to economic problems in Europe, the methods disappeared somewhat, leaving only those riders who were last formed at their country's school. Most of those riders and trainers are now gone and all that is left is what they wrote. What I write here is not comparable. But if I can motivate the modern dedicated horsemen to read what has been written, this vast quantity of learning need not be lost.

It must also be said that the breeding of horses is no longer as regional as it was at the beginning. All national interests have been made more flexible and a mixture of breeds is often used to produce the modern sport horse. This type of horse is faster and more sensitive than the original models. The original methods were certainly based on the breed of the horse produced in the country. Over time, riding has become much more universal in nature. However, horses still fall into categories and a good basic knowledge of the philosophy of each classical method is a huge advantage when faced with many different types of horses. The method of riding is always determined by the horse.

With this objective in mind, I invite you to read on...

♊

CHAPTER ONE
IT BEGAN WITH A DEAL

As a little girl, I was very shy. I didn't talk. I avoided the obligation of social obligations by reading. The only talking I did was to the groups of horses and ponies along the fence lines on my walks in White Bear Lake, Minnesota, where I grew up. I made flowers out of tissue paper and fastened them to the halters or manes of my favorites, using bobby pins from my mother's dressing table. And I told everything to these horses!

When the pony bit me, I was shocked. There was blood. I had no idea that the owner of the pony had been watching me from his window. There he was, quickly at my side, along the fence.

"Little girl," he said. "Come into the house and we will wash that bite and fix you up just fine!" He spoke in an Irish way and was very polite. After the band-aids were in place, he said, "Now, if you promise not to tell your father about my pony having bitten you, I will show you how to ride that pony."

I stared at the ground for about five seconds before I could say, "That's a deal."

My life with horses began with a deal. This deal was with Maurice Roberts, a horse dealer from the Chicago area, who had transplanted to Minnesota to start a new business in horse sales. He made good on his deal by providing me with a small bridle, putting it on the pony's head for the first time, and giving me a bit of Irish wisdom: "Take a deep seat, a long holt, and don't let him see you."

Completely mystified by those words, I climbed on, by way of the water trough, and proceeded to learn about Shetland ponies. The pony would only move in the direction of the water trough where he was fed. So, I immediately got off. I led the pony about fifty feet away, climbed back on, and enjoyed a first ride back to the trough!

As the days went on, I found that the further I led the pony away from the trough, the faster he went on the return trip. After one month, I could lead him to the far end of the pasture, get on, and fly! Unfortunately, this ended the day that he flew to the trough and dropped his head at the very last minute, neatly depositing me into the water. Twice lucky, Mr. Roberts was nearby and saw me rising out of the trough, completely soaked. He came over and told me that he would show me how to ride a horse. My life began with that decision on his part. I was eleven years old, and he and his horses became my life.

As I could walk to the stable, I rode before school as well as after school. As I became better and more useful to Mr. Roberts, he loaned me his farm-registered Jeep to drive to school, so I could be at the stable earlier. In Minnesota, at twelve years old, one has the right to drive a farm-registered vehicle.

The horses were taught to jump in the chute, free. But Mr. Roberts believed that this should be done carrying a rider. That was me! Mostly, what he taught me was to *"Sit chilly,"* or quietly and calmly, so as not to disturb the horse. The jumping course, built in the grass ring, never changed. So when I was given a bridle, there was still not much to do, as the horses memorized the course very quickly. Within a year, I was riding in the local shows, and Mr. Roberts was selling horses!

My family was not involved in horses in any way, but they finally bought a horse for my Christmas present, from Mr. Roberts, for $500. He was worth every penny. Mr. Roberts remained sure that I would ride his horses in the competitions because mine was a non-starter. In the end, my father doubled his investment, and Mr. Roberts found me a horse. As the horse was an absolute runaway if one did not sit very chilly, I could ride him where others had failed. I left the horse completely alone. He won everything in that area for years.

This horse, Mr O'Malley, had a particular and infallible manner of judging the takeoff point for the jump. Four strides before the jump, he would set himself up, imperceptibly. Then, he would march those four strides to the jump, always getting a fine distance. Years later, upon my arrival in Massachusetts with O'Malley, I came across a judge, Norman Hall, who had judged me in the Chicago area whilst riding him. He told me that he and the other judges at the show all commented on this and they thought he was a great horse because of that. Certainly, it helped me to learn to find the distances on all the other horses I was riding. I had to learn to trust O'Malley and to not move in the saddle. His type of personality became my favorite kind of horse to ride for all of my life.

My system of passivity, which served me well on many horses in my life, proved to not be the complete solution to horse mastership when we went to the bigger shows. My first experience at Lake Forest, Illinois, where one jumped out of the ring onto the outside course and then back into the ring at the end, was a disaster. Mr. Roberts put me on a beautiful black, who was a very good mover and jumper, and slid me into the ring. We did not warm up. I never asked questions. We jumped out of the ring beautifully and galloped onto the rest of the course. I rapidly realized that I had no control and that I was on a runaway. I also knew better than to let this be known to the spectators. I sat very chilly, hoping that the length of the course would tire the horse. It was not so. We increased speed over every jump until we turned to jump into the ring to finish in front of the grandstand. By this time, people were on their feet. I jumped into the ring brilliantly and flew past the grandstand, where I saw two people making the sign of the cross!

At that time, it was commonplace to have an In Gate and an Out Gate at shows to avoid unruly horses in a small area and confrontations between unhappy trainers. This saved my life that day, as my horse saw the Out Gate, and with no break in stride, flew directly to it and jumped out of the ring. We disappeared into the stabling area, where he found his stall. There was nowhere to hide, so I sat down and waited for Mr. Roberts and the end of my career.

Saved again, Mr. Roberts came into the stable accompanied by Max Bonham, a well-known rider and trainer at the time. Max was carrying a bridle and scolding Mr. Roberts for having put me on such a horse. He adjusted the new bridle to the horse and told Mr. Roberts that I was to ride the next day with the new polo bit. I had never seen such a bit. The horse was easy the next day, I did not lose my career, and I will forever be thankful to Max Bonham. He was more than a horseman.

Mr. Roberts was constantly on the lookout for inexpensive horses to improve and then sell. His imagination led him to buy a gray, overgrown pony from the rodeo, where Mr. Roberts was a spectator at the Saddle Bronc event. He believed that the horse could jump as he was a very good bucker. He did not confide the pony's history to anyone as he would then have to shoulder the responsibility. But he didn't have to. His instinct was right! Once the bucking strap was removed, bucking was the furthest thing from Silver's mind. And he could really jump. Renamed Little Squire, after one of Mr. Roberts' favorites in the past, I competed him in both horsemanship and jumper competitions, and he took care of me.

Another one of Mr. Roberts' experiments was less fruitful. The huge overpopulation of Mustang horses in the West gave rise to a government program for their dispersal. If one agreed to take 10 horses, the government would ship them by rail to the nearest livestock yard to the buyer. For us, this was the Minneapolis Livestock Yard. The buyer paid $10 for each of the 10 horses once they were loaded on the truck. For two years, in the fall, Mr. Roberts took his truck to the stockyards and came home with 10 wild, unkempt, poorly fed horses with big heads. He turned them out in the big field. We did not ride all winter as the climate was impossible and the horses were turned out and unclipped. Having little to do, I would go out into the field and crouch down in the middle, in the snow, to wait for the natural curiosity of the horses to bring them to me. Sometimes, this would take three days of sitting in the snow. In the end, I would be sitting in the middle of the herd. Later, Mr. Roberts told me that he watched me from the window.

In the spring, the mustangs would be brought in to be broken to saddle and to be free-jumped. This would help us find out if there were any candidates for competition horses in the herd. Mr. Roberts' nephews, who were very good riders, broke the mustangs in. If there was one that was too difficult for them, it was sent to the nearby Indian reservation, where it would work in harness between two big draft horses pulling logs. After a month, the horse would come home ready to continue its education, but in a sad state. I felt very bad about this. We did end up with a few horses that worked out.

In that era, the Indians from the reservation were available as a workforce under strict regulation. The government paid a part of their salary and they were to receive housing on top of a salary. No liquor was permitted to be in their possession at any time. Working on a horse farm was a great change for them and we liked to have them. I got two of them in trouble...

In the winter, on Saturday mornings, we all watched Western movies on television instead of riding. Cowboys fascinated me. It was often part of the story that the cowboy would jump off the second-story roof onto a waiting horse tied below, and make his escape at a full gallop. This was something I wanted to try. We had a loft door for the hay delivery positioned directly above the main door into the barn. There was a large cement floor in front of the entry, which was kept very well swept.

One day, I noticed that Mr. Roberts' car was gone when I arrived at the stable. I seized the opportunity to position a horse on the cement slab below the loft door, with two Indians holding it precisely in place. Then, I ran up the ladder inside to get into the hayloft and opened the hayloft door. The horse spooked and bolted, dragging the two Indians out onto the yard, making a lot of noise. I got them back in position and got ready to jump. I had seen this done a lot and I felt I knew how to do it. So... I leaped! I landed on the saddle, the horse slid on the slippery cement, and we both fell flat on the ground.

I yelled very loudly at the pain of landing on the saddle, and the Indians, who had no idea that I was going to jump, yelled at me at great volume too. It turns out that the stuntmen land on their hands and knees, and slide down into the saddle. I leaped with my legs wide apart and landed sitting in a full seat. Terrible pain! It was a catastrophe. But worse, coming out of the door of the house was Mr. Roberts. His car had been taken for repairs and he was watching from the window. I was thrown out of the stable and had a long and painful walk home. It must be said that I was thrown out periodically for my antics. But, after three weeks, Mr. Roberts would call my father and say that I could come back if I could behave.

Mr. Roberts had a beautiful gray mare that I was allowed to ride. I always rode in my cowboy hat and boots. She wasn't much of a jumper but I taught her to rear. She was dramatic when she reared as she pawed the air with her front feet. I tried to take off my hat and wave it at the height of the rear. One day, when my boss was away looking for horses, there was the High School Homecoming Parade in White Bear Lake. I love parades and I always wanted to ride in one. So I did. I rode the gray mare to the parade, in my hat and boots, wishing I had a western saddle, and joined it. Whenever we stopped, I made the mare rear up and I took off my hat. It was going great until we stopped at an intersection where cars were stopped, waiting for the parade to pass. I reared and I waved. There he was, in the first car: Mr. Roberts, on his way home. He jumped out and pointed at the way home without saying a word. Naturally, I walked home and was thrown out again for three weeks. My sense of adventure got me in trouble.

I rode constantly at Erin Vale, with Maurice Roberts, for three years. There, I met Kate Butler, whose father, Patrick Butler, was the owner of some wonderful horses, like Balbuco, who were donated to the U.S. jumping team. I also met and rode with the Parrish family, as well as Robert Powers and his wife, Zandra, who were my friends. I also rode with Mr. Roberts' nephews and niece, as well as his brother Mike, who also spent hours trying to teach me.

When my parents decided to move back to their home ground of Boston, I was sad to leave. My family had moved to Minnesota so that we kids could have our childhood there. It was at an end. My brother, who had graduated from St. Paul Academy with honors, was accepted to Princeton. I had one more year to go in high school. I felt a little lost.

Chapter One

CHAPTER TWO
UPROOTED

The long drive from Minnesota to Massachusetts, with just my mother and me, was a moment of uncertainty. My father had gone before us to start his work and my mother did not drive. So I was the one to drive across the country in the winter at the age of 15. I was leaving my horse behind until we found a new home in Massachusetts and a stable nearby. I was to restart school as soon as that was accomplished. Nothing was sure.

My mother and I were commissioned to find the house, while my father was reorganizing his research department at The Kendall Company. He gave us strict limitations of how far he would commute to work, and that he would drive to the west in the morning and to the east at the end of the day. I got a map out and used a compass to make a big circle around the area we were to focus on. I could not be enrolled in school until we found a new house so I was very picky. We found a huge house with old established trees and a lovely old barn in Framingham. It had a lovely huge country kitchen, a library for my father, and two living rooms. It had all one could ask. We bought it, and my request to keep my horse at home was quickly denied. Consequently, I began school and went in search of a place to keep my horse.

I found Millwood Hunt Club, which was not far, so arrangements were made for Mr O'Malley, my horse and best friend, to have a stall. I knew no one at the club and nothing about fox hunting or hounds. The problem of transport seemed an impossibility during the winter, and I was very sad. I was saved by the generosity of Richard Cheska, a friend of Mr. Roberts and a kind man who always gave me good advice. Richard was the father of Donald and Robert Cheska, among five children.

These boys became very well-known in the horse show world later. He volunteered to make the drive with a two-horse trailer and my horse. I will never forget his kindness in taking on such a trip just to get me my horse. He took the southern route, as the northern route via the Canadian highway was considered too risky during December. All the same, the trip took over a week, and I was spared the details.

When O'Malley arrived at Millwood Hunt Club, he was an immediate celebrity. I came to the stable after school to find him safely arrived and surrounded by curious members of the club. His stall door was opened and he was being photographed—not for his fame as a competitor but for his winter coat! In Minnesota, the horses were turned out for the winter, without blankets. They grew huge coats and assumed a Neanderthal look. He looked huge, due to the long hair and feathers, with his head almost hidden. No one had ever witnessed this in Massachusetts and he was visited every day by the curious. I was so proud of him. He was my ticket to meet people!

Eventually, the kind Yummy Albright, who ran the club's stable, arranged to have him clipped. This was to my regret as I thought he looked beautiful in his winter robe. As he was about 10 years old and it was the first time in his life that he was clipped, he was tranquilized. I bought a blanket and he became a civilized member of the club. It seemed so warm to me compared with Minnesota that I rarely wore a coat.

I soon discovered that the method of riding preferred at the Millwood Hunt Club, taught by Vladimir Littauer, was an offshoot of the Caprilli Method. With a sigh of relief, I quickly adapted to a method that I had studied in books but had never seen in practice. I met Honora Haynes, Paul Cronin, Charlie Collins, and Janet Stevens, who all rode strictly in that method. I followed suit. O'Malley was a horse to leave alone so that was not much difference to him. When it became apparent that I knew and could duplicate what was acceptable in this new stable, I was so relieved. We were found! Paul, especially, was very kind in further explaining the fine points of this wonderful Italian method of riding. As the American hunter style of riding is an evolution of the Caprilli method, all that I learned and copied was useful to me in later hunter competitions. My horse was truly adapted to this way of riding. Later, Paul went on to direct the riding program at Sweet Briar College for 34 years.

All was well for a time as I rode at the club, but with no trainer and no transport, there was no opportunity to compete. However, at the end of the following summer, I was approached as a possible representative of Millwood Hunt Club. I was asked to ride in the New England Field Hunter Championship, held in the early fall. I had never hunted, nor had O'Malley, but we accepted. I was instructed on what would be required at the competition. We would jump a cross-country hunting type course and do other tests to show that O'Malley was a good field hunter. The day arrived and O'Malley was perfectly happy to jump all those little jumps in the woods and the fields. In the end, we received a huge trophy to keep for a year, as the new Champion Field Hunter of New England!

O'Malley was a real champion and had given me everything. However, without the constant care of Mr. Roberts on a tendon which was always the weak point of my horse, he was at the end of his performance life. I left him with a friend as I left for my first semester at St. Lawrence University. We agreed, O'Malley and I, that he had reached retirement. Suddenly, I was on foot!

During my time at the Millwood Hunt Club, I had met my future husband, Richard Ulrich, who was then riding for Mrs. Gardner Fiske. Mrs. Fiske rode sidesaddle. Richard was obliged to occasionally do the same to ensure that her horses were well-schooled. I found this very amusing! He really loved dressage and had ridden under Captain Fred Marsman, who was the head of the Dana Hall Riding Department. Richard was his protégé and had a real feeling for this type of riding. I had read a lot about both the French and the German methods but had never seen any dressage, other than in photographs. Having adopted the Littauer method to be the acceptable method at the Club, my riding was unacceptable to Richard. Even then, the politics within the sport started to become apparent.

When I started at St. Lawrence, I loved it. But I missed my horse and my riding terribly. I have always enjoyed school and reading, but I came to the decision that I could do that on my own. I had to decide if I would be a journalist or a rider. As Richard and I decided to marry, I dropped out. My family was aghast. My life as a writer went on hold. I became a professional rider and my real life began.

CHAPTER THREE
THE FIRST NEW BEGINNING

When Richard married me, he thought that he was marrying a partner, a right-hand girl. But, because of my upbringing, he had a surprise coming. I had never made a bed, ironed a shirt, or made a cup of coffee in my life. At college, I had paid the girl next door to tidy my dorm room so that it passed inspection. I had also paid her to do my ironing. The first dinner I made for Richard was macaroni and cheese. It was served in the lovely silver tureen we received at our wedding, and accompanied by the solid silver serving fork coming from the same source. It was beautiful as I brought it to the table which I had set myself. There were two forks, two spoons, folded linen napkins, two glasses at each of our places, and candles. He tried to serve the macaroni but was unable to push the fork into the casserole. He tried again without further success. Then, he looked at me and asked, *"Did you remember to cook the macaroni first?"* I burst into tears. I had a long way to go.

It wasn't much better in the stable. I could ride. Under stress, I could also saddle and bridle a horse. Other than that, I could not do too much. I did not know what to feed, when to give hay, or how to drive a wheelbarrow. In my home, my father refused to consider that a woman should be employed. I had never had a job. But I could sit chilly on a hot horse!

Richard was already the owner of a summer stable, Dennis Riding School, on Cape Cod, which opened in mid-June and closed on Labor Day. It was assumed that I would be ready to muck out stalls, groom horses, and teach all day every day for the full duration. I had a lot to learn but I was thrilled! My first job!

As Richard had a full-time job running a stable near Boston, I went to run Dennis Riding School with Richard's brother and two sisters. Luckily, one of his sisters did the cooking. I rapidly learned to do the rest. I led trail rides and taught camp riders and other tourists all day long. Richard's older brother, Donald, also taught and groomed like me, but he didn't know how to ride. As he was a school teacher during the winter, liked to act, and was charming, he had all the prerequisites for a beginner-level riding instructor. He also handled the money very carefully.

A part of the challenge of a summer stable is that one must lease the horses to use in the school and, in our case, on the trail rides. Also in our case, as we handled all of the summer camp riding programs on Cape Cod, we needed horses for Seascape Camp for overweight girls. These horses needed to be weight carriers, not too tall (in case of the inevitable spill), and slow. We could only have 12 horses with our budget. All of our horses did all the jobs. Jumping was pretty much out of the question.

Most of the horses remained saddled all day and went out four to five times. We fed a lot and three times a day. They all gained weight, a point stressed by Richard. I learned to saddle and pad a horse in such a way that he could work every day. Richard never leased poorly conformed horses to avoid having a difficult horse to saddle. Today, I never buy a horse that does not carry a saddle well. Horses that need breastplates or ponies that need cruppers could never get past Richard's scrutiny. We used endurance-type saddles that spread the weight over a large surface. All saddles fit exactly the horse assigned. Richard added and adjusted the padding, and the girths and saddles were not changed during the day. All girths were rope girths. We never had sore backs and that was very important with a small group of horses. They worked hard.

We had no electricity so Coleman lanterns came into use if you were still awake after sundown. I was in a different world and pretty tired by the end of a successful summer. Being out of favor with my family made me realize what a privileged life I had led as a child. Now, Richard and I were on a strict budget and we saved every penny. We tried to get invitations to dinner to make ends meet. After the summer, we could think about buying a winter stable to build ourselves. Richard found just the spot.

I was 18 when we bought our first farm in Pembroke, Massachusetts. Friars Gate Farm was a back lot with a cabin, on a hillside covered
with trees. The farm cost $15,000 and we had to apply for a mortgage.
We also had to clear the land, get rid of the tree stumps, and build a barn.
I was eager to begin! I was eager to have O'Malley back from the friends
who had kept him for me and give him his own stall.

Richard found a day job working in Boston with his father, and I
worked alone during the day sawing trees. Richard cut and stacked the
wood after work and on weekends. After the first two days, he was not
happy with my work. The trees fell in every direction and were on top
of each other. It was impossible to sort out the mess. I had to learn how
to control the direction of the fall of the tree that I cut. I was not a great
assistant but I was always energetic. I had only a hand saw. It was my first
wedding anniversary present from Richard. He decided that I was not
ready for a chainsaw... rightly so.

I was born with my father's energy. My father was a chemist and a
very smart man. He was a Harvard graduate who drove a cab all night to
work his way through his studies. He invented many diverse things in his
life while employed by The Kendall Company and Raymond Laboratories.
For example, he was responsible for inventing the Toni Home Permanent
and a non-woven tissue for disposable diapers. His curiosity and inventive personality permeated our family and he encouraged diversity in all
that we did. He was the Vice President in charge of Research, but was
never happy with the sales department at Kendall Mills, as his inventions
were, in his eyes, poorly marketed. He asked to be, in addition to his Research department position, the Vice President in charge of sales. So, he
was given two offices, two secretaries, and two departments to run. He
had energy. When I was a very small girl, he told me, as I looked straight
up to listen closely, that I could be whatever I wanted to be if I tried. I
believed everything that he told me.

I have always believed that one is born with one major gift from God.
The first few years are spent discovering that gift. It can be beauty, which
is a shame because that is fleeting. It can be intelligence, athleticism, talent, endurance, intuition, or, as in my case, energy. The second phase
of life is to find a way to use this gift. I did this through my passion for

horses and hard work. My gift has served me well. I am never tired. I have had some working students with the same energy and it is always fun to discover. I have learned that energy is greatly enhanced by hope and by progress. An optimist is always more energetic than a pessimist.

In the modern day, it is common to complain about the lack of energy and drive in our youth. I have found this to be a direct result of a sense of hopelessness or frustration. Both hopelessness and frustration are eliminated by achievement and progress. It is important to have a goal in the short term and the means and the help to accomplish that goal. Energy and optimism will follow directly.

I finally learned to make the trees fall in parallel fashion, and Richard began to establish the location of the first barn. We drew pictures of that barn to prepare for the construction. A gambrel roof was our choice. It was to have seventeen stalls, a tack room, a feed room, and lots of room in the hayloft due to the shape of that roof. I was to learn a lot about construction. The bulldozer came when the plot was cleared to dig the footings, which I was to fill with rocks in order to use less cement. In New England, there are plenty of rocks and I used a wheelbarrow to do the best I could. O'Malley was getting closer.

This barn was the first of many that we built, and it was a learning experience. We first used "tongue and groove"-style boards to build the stalls, and had to do it all over again. It seemed the horses easily dismantled these stalls so Richard decided to pour a cement footing between each stall. He laid a row of cement blocks upon that footing and then framed the wall to sit on these blocks. Each side of that wall was covered with oak boards. The lesson we learned from this very first barn is that one must build to withstand the years. There is a parallel lesson to be learned in training a horse, building a ring, or repairing a horse van. It all must be built to withstand the years. The worst loss of time is the time spent redoing what was poorly done at the beginning.

O'Malley's box was box number one in this barn. He was certainly a horse of my lifetime, and he was living through this transition with me. We had been winners, written up in the newspapers, and applauded in seven states. Now, it was time to earn our keep. O'Malley was to become a carefully used school horse.

We had one client when we opened Friars Gate Farm and he was given the privilege of riding O'Malley. He came from Washington, D.C., to Boston each weekend, where he lived with his wife and son. Francis Shea was a lawyer with vast experience. He had helped to organize the Nuremberg War Trials. He had argued in front of the Supreme Court, representing the Southern Railroads. His wife had danced in the Metropolitan Ballet in New York. Mr. Shea appreciated the gesture we made to teach him on my wonderful horse. I felt that both O'Malley and I had turned over a new page and we began to live a responsible life.

CHAPTER FOUR
BUYING AT THE SALES

B uying horses at an auction was a great adventure, and was a big part of our early endeavors to find suitable horses to train in our newly constructed stable. I had never been to a horse auction when I married Richard, so he led the way as we made various experiments.

Close to home, in Milton, Massachusetts, Bushy's Auction was held every Tuesday night. All sorts of horses, including those destined for slaughter, were sent through a narrow corridor into the sales ring. Those suitable to be ridden were ridden. That presented my first public appearance in the auction world, as the owners of these horses would scan the crowd to find riders to present the horses. When in the sales ring, the auctioneer always announced that it was the horse and not the girl that was being sold. Every week he got a laugh with this line! I was honored to be asked and was quickly thrown up onto a horse. Richard was surprised to see me show up in a western saddle on a pretty, skinny bay. We were sold for around $500, and Richard followed us out to make sure I did not persist in that activity.

Further afield, we attended Bunchy Grant Auction somewhere in New Jersey. It was a more sophisticated crowd. One had to scrutinize the horse carefully to see which parts were missing, or that the age of the horse corresponded with the teeth of the horse. It was at this sale that I saw Geraldine, the bidder for AmFran Horse Buyers. Those that she bought were shipped to France as horses for slaughter. She could tell the weight and category of a horse with a blink of an eye, and I was fascinated. The big, rawboned horses were less appealing to her than the short, round type. The category was more important than the weight, I learned. Richard said that if one could calculate exactly as she did, one already had the base price of the horse passing through. I studied very hard. Richard was a special type of buyer. This was all new to me. I was learning the practical side of horse life.

The New Holland Auction, in the heart of the Amish country, was colorful, and, in my opinion, had the best quality horses. In order to go, we had to leave right after feeding our horses and drive very fast. After one of those top-speed trips, we raced into the sales area to see a handsome, tall gelding being led around the ring. We watched as the bidding stopped within our price range. Richard threw up his hand and we owned a horse!

As we had not registered as buyers, we were escorted to the auctioneer to make arrangements to pay. He looked us over. He thought for a moment, then asked Richard why he would buy a blind horse. We had arrived after the announcement that the horse, with two dark brown eyes, was sightless. The auctioneer patted me on the shoulder, lightly punched Richard on the arm, and told us to be more careful. We did not pay for the blind horse.

The most memorable auction for me was the Kinloch Farm Auction. It was a private affair after the tragic death of the owners, the Currier family, in the Bermuda Triangle. It was a dispersal sale of Andalusians and Welsh ponies. Our good friend, Ray LeBlanc, who loved to buy and sell anything, told us that we must all fly down to Washington to attend this historic sale. Ray said that he would handle the details. This should have raised flags. When we met at Boston Logan Airport, Ray was wearing a black Nehru-collared jacket and black slacks. He looked a little like a priest. Richard and I were dressed appropriately for a country auction. As we landed in Washington, we found that Ray had rented a huge black Cadillac with tinted windows in which we were to drive to the sale at Kinloch. He sat in the front. We were in the back seat. I began to feel ostentatious.

When we arrived at the auction, Ray declared that he would stand apart from us. As the sale went along, I suddenly saw Ray across the way, standing taller than the crowd in his black outfit. He looked a little like Abraham Lincoln in that setting. And he was bidding! I nudged

Richard as the hammer went down and Ray signed for the purchase of a huge Andalusian mare. We looked at each other and shook our heads. However, as the afternoon went on, Ray kept buying more. He bought another gray Andalusian mare and a total of three Welsh ponies. Each time he signed, smiling, as people near him began to congratulate him. As the sale drew to a close and we stood up to leave and drive to the airport, the auctioneer called us to attention to appreciate the top buyer of the sale: Richard Ulrich! Great applause rang out, as Ray, on his seat in his Nehru jacket, waved and then discreetly made the sign of the cross. Richard was frozen to his place, realizing that Ray had signed Richard Ulrich on all the paperwork.

Back in Massachusetts, we went to work to try to find buyers for the Andalusian mares. They couldn't jump. I tried. Eventually, one went as a donation to a Catholic mission in Peru to deliver mail. I think Alex Dunaif, a very young student at the time, convinced her mother to very kindly take the other. We easily disposed of the Welsh ponies. We never took Ray with us to another auction.

Auction buying was a favorite pastime for Richard, and I was to train the horses he found. He went to many auctions in Missouri, Illinois, and Ohio, and found a lot of nice horses. Even more accessible than the auction circuit was the daily possibility of going up and down the shed rows at the New England racetracks to ask for horses for sale. Most of our horses came from the racetrack and were very happy with their new lives. My students always had access to plenty of projects from both sources and it was good for their education.

Many of these reclaimed racehorses went on to be at the top level in dressage, due to Karl Mikolka's influence, as well as in the hunter and jumper disciplines. The most important quality in these unknown horses was their soundness. Any horse, being sound, can be trained to do high-level dressage and can also be taught to jump, within his limit. Years later, Reiner Klimke told me that it takes three years to achieve the Grand Prix level if one starts with a basically trained mature horse. But, he specified, only a certain number of them would be beautiful enough to compete. The others are like workbooks in school, to be filled in carefully, but not to be exhibited.

RIDING LESSON

At the beginning of the story is the process of selecting the horse with which to make the journey toward the goal you have set. There are a few old adages to apply, before getting down to details: no one has a crystal ball; only invest in a horse the sum which you can afford to lose; and, the perfect horse does not exist. Other volumes have been written and other lists of characteristics of a good horse have been made, all of which have good points. Here is yet another point of view.

The selection of a possible candidate with which to begin is based on the analysis of that candidate in several aspects. Imperfections, or areas of weakness, are important in direct proportion to the possibility of their correction.

Begin with a good look at the horse from the side to appraise his skeleton. This cannot be changed, although a very young horse, as it matures, will change somewhat in a predictable manner. There are certain skeletal types which can do one job more easily than another, so it is important to know the goal being set for each horse. For example, a horse with a neck set low on the shoulder, with strong hindquarters, is a type which may win the Arc de Triomphe race but may find a vertical of 1.50m or a pirouette a huge challenge.

A long wither and a long sloping shoulder, and a big and equilateral triangle formed by the structure of the hindquarters (hip-point of buttocks-stifle), are important points. There should be a horizontal line between the mouth of the horse and the point of the buttocks which is parallel with the ground. Good balance is important for longevity in most disciplines. The racehorse can be built downhill for speed, but to use this wonderful breed as an eventer or as a jumper, the balance must be correct.

The skeleton must be examined from all angles and very carefully. This will not change. Immature horses are the hardest to judge, and there are experts who can see a foal or a yearling, but who stay away from two-

THE SELECTION PROCESS

year-olds as being impossible to judge. From three years old, when the wither is defined, it is easier to judge.

The old adage, "Fat hides a lot of sins," is accurate. It is easier to judge the skeletal construction of a normally fit horse. The importance of the skeleton is impossible to overestimate. A short blunt shoulder with a neck set on the lower part of that shoulder will be a problem for life. It cannot be offset by a big and strong hindquarter if one is to approach the higher levels. The right skeleton will produce efficient movement. Efficient movement enables longevity.

The horse with correct legs and good feet will outlast his crooked brother. Racehorses sometimes run only a year or two before going to the breeding shed. Sometimes, these horses stay sound that long with imperfect alignment, and are then used in breeding. That is a shame. In most disciplines, horses are used for 10 to 15 years. Poorly constructed horses usually become uncomfortable or lame long before they age out.

The second look at this candidate should be an analysis of his muscles. At five years or more, his muscles tell the tale of how he functions and of how well he is holding up to his training program. The ideal age at which to choose a horse is five or more because of this aspect. The muscle should be laid on uniformly over the whole horse. An area of no muscle will show a horse not functioning correctly. No topline, an ewe neck, or weak thighs all signify a potential lameness or a poor training program. A potential lameness may be apparent at the later movement analysis. Imperfect muscling due to a poor training program can be corrected. At this point, and to make a final analysis of the horse, it is necessary to move to the third look, his movement.

I begin with the horse in controlled liberty—that is, on a longe or in a jumping round—where I can see the gaits I wish to see:

The Walk: The length of the overstep should be six to eight inches. This is terribly important. The walk is a cousin to the canter and all the faults of the canter are to be seen at the walk. A lesser overstep is evidence of a shorter than usual stride. Scope is an important factor in longevity. The walk should also have four distinct beats and no tendency to pace. Pacing at the walk tends to produce a four-beat canter which is weaker when collected. The walk deserves a good look.

The Trot: Any horse can do a working trot, and the hind hoof must land easily in the print made by the front hoof on the same side at this trot. Overstepping is less serious than not achieving this length of stride easily. The balance of the horse is never better than that displayed at the trot. There should be an imaginary line drawn between the mouth of the horse and the point of the buttocks. That line should be horizontal.

The Canter: A really important factor for me is that the horse prefers the canter to the trot. His hind leg, on the inside, should land under the seat of the rider. On a 20-meter circle with no side reins, there should be no sign of disuniting behind, especially the last stride of the canter before passing into the trot. The cadence moment, or the moment of suspension, should be easily identified but not exaggerated. The canter should be pure and of easy balance.

To see the horse ridden at the three gaits will make visible his reaction to the weight and the constraint of a rider. Problems with a rider that did not exist without the rider are usually perfected by a change of method. Problems preexisting in liberty, not so much.

To me, a horse should change his leads naturally, with little training, as he did as a young horse. In the flying change, one can see the tendencies at the jump, such as the loss of balance, anxiety, undue acceleration, and loss of hind leg function. So, it is important to see the flying change.

Jumping analysis is most valuable when done with a rider. Many mistakes are made by prejudging a horse in liberty who changes his technique dramatically with the weight of a rider. The technique should be good from the start. Good use of the shoulder, correct time spent in the air, landing on each lead, and good use of the back. The height of the jump is less important than the style. The horse should focus, and back up if necessary, but not spook overly at a Liverpool or a flower box. If he exaggerates a good technique over a jump, which is visually impressive, he gets bonus points.

The fourth and most important look, or consideration, that must now be done is the analysis of character. This will be the deciding factor for the training and formation of the horse. The character should mesh with the rider or trainer. Do not start with a conflict of character. The character cannot be changed. The horse can be educated. His character will remain the same. If he is not liked by his handlers, he will not succeed. Some people like mares, some do not. Pick what corresponds with the program and the rider or trainer. Take into consideration the effect of the work the horse will do. A horse with a huge ego and self-assured naïveté will settle rapidly with the right gymnastic work over jumps. The same horse, in dressage, can be a bit of a bear for the first part of his training. In order to analyze the character, a two-week trial is ideal, or a long talk with his recent rider if no trial is possible.

The real work begins once you have made your choice. There is no bad choice if you invest all of your energies to justify that choice. There is no perfect horse. Choose wisely, work very carefully, and work hard. Do the best that you can to make the horse reach his potential. You cannot go further than his potential. Good luck!

CHAPTER FIVE
BUILDING A FUTURE

I n the end, we built, more or less in the same fashion as we had built our first barn, stabling for 115 horses and a huge indoor arena. It took a few years. Richard's theory of paying as you go, with no building loans, endeared him to my New England father. My parents realized that the marriage would really go on and they began to visit after an absence of about five years. During those five years, I had learned a lot about working. I was very happy.

I learned to set cement blocks, assemble the huge roof trusses from Unadilla Silo Company for the roof of the indoor ring, and paint. One of Richard's friends from high school was a bricklayer. He showed me how to place the blocks and how to finish the mortar. He told Richard that I could lay the same number of blocks as allowed by the union in only a few weeks of training. As this illustrated, the unions were based on the slowest worker. Thank goodness we did not have any union workers on our site. Instead, we had owner-workers! The days were long but the progress was fast.

Richard bought two buildings that were moved onto the property: a motel unit for help to live in and a larger garage which was set on a hill. The latter was to become a two-story building with the stable below and the clubhouse above. My billiard table had a home! My stress-releasing hobby of playing billiards, learned from my father, turned out to be very popular with older students and parents waiting for their children in long afternoon lessons. At the time, Shell Oil decided to change its colors, and huge barrels of bright yellow paint were suddenly practically given away. Richard bought many barrels, gave one bucket and one roller brush to each student, and told them to paint. Soon, the inside of the barns and the indoor were all a cheerful yellow! Richard was always on the lookout for clever ways to save money.

We bought 48,000 pounds of Maine poultry oats in one of his schemes. They were delivered by two Maine farmers in 80-pound sacks labeled "Maine Potatoes." Richard sold all these oats to our friends in the area at a fraction of what we were all used to paying. In addition, one of the Maine farmers liked the farm so much that he applied for a job as a maintenance man. He brought his wife and moved into the original cabin. Richard's schemes were becoming a topic of conversation.

I gradually began to ride in competition again, and students arrived at the farm to take lessons, and then lease or buy horses, to be part of the Friars Gate rider team. Our junior students were like our family, as in so many stables of that era, and they stayed all day whenever they could. They helped with stalls, grooming, raking, building, and riding extra horses. Coming from farther away, students could stay overnight in our spare bedroom. My cooking improved somewhat, but Richard made a lot of spaghetti sauce...

One of Richard's many strong points was his ability to see a sound horse. He bought medium quality horses but very sound ones. This gave me the time to train them long enough to get to an interesting level with a still sound animal. As I didn't know a lot about training, it took me longer at the beginning, but I had a lot of good advice from the older professionals around me.

During this time, I also rode a lot. In the morning, I always started with four of the horses that were being used in afternoon lessons by their junior owners. This was in memory of Mr. Roberts who prepared my horses while I was at school. Then, I rode 10 more. I found that if I got onto the first horse at 4:30 a.m., I could be done riding and ready to teach at 2:30 p.m. when the kids arrived from school. I could teach until 6 p.m. when the parents came and took them away. The students who were more advanced rode in one lesson and then rode another horse whose name was on their list on "The Day Sheet." "The Day Sheet" was impressive. I did this every day, except Mondays and show days, for 20 years.

We needed horses for my juniors to buy as projects and to take to shows. My best friends Ralph and Holly Caristo had a sales and training barn on Long Island and were willing to send horses on a trial basis for the kids to try. Ralph sent his daughters to my camp and was a huge support to me as a new professional. Holly was an artist and also an avid competitor in jumper divisions. She loved Quarter Horses as jumpers and did the big Quarter Horse Congress competition every year in Columbus, Ohio.

This is a marathon competition of Quarter Horses in every manner. The show runs all night long, with junior classes lasting eight hours at times. Holly had too many to ride one year and I was thrilled to be asked to ride one of her horses in the jumper class. The one I rode was a giant in comparison with a normal Quarter Horse. I had to trot to the combination as the distances were all measured for a smaller, typical Quarter Horse. In the schooling area, there was only one jump. There was a wooden coop about two feet tall, and a rail held by two cowboys. The cowboys held the rail over the coop at whatever height one wanted. Genial! I watched the show until about 1:30 a.m. and then went to bed. It was a real adventure and worth the 10-hour drive to remote western Ohio.

Over the years, we bought some wonderful horses from Ralph and Holly. One day, Ralph called to ask me to come down to Long Island to buy a horse. He did not say to try a horse. When I arrived, I commented on this, and he told me that I had no choice. I rode the horse, a Quarter Horse with a short step and feisty personality. I found him to be very careful but really not my type. I had no choice. Ralph insisted. Turns out, Ralph was right. Bunker Hill was one of the best horses I ever bought! After I sold him on, he ended up winning the speed class at the Newport Derby with Jamie Mann. Ralph and Holly were often my best advisors.

Malcolm Gladwell, *The New Yorker* columnist who wrote multiple books including *What The Dog Saw*, wrote that it takes 10,000 hours of practice to become competent in any field. He used The Beatles and Bill Gates as examples and told their stories well. He could have told mine. I learned slowly and I learned from the horses I had. I read voraciously, and I bought the book of dressage tests to use as my guideline, as one could rarely see upper level dressage being practiced in the United States in that era.

Richard bought the horses. He searched at the racetracks and at auctions. Then, he discovered the PMU (Pregnant Mare Urine) program in Ontario. Mares were bred, then stood in stanchions, like cows, with rubber collection hoses fixed onto them to collect their urine. Every week, this urine was sent away to a laboratory where an extract was used to produce hormone replacement therapy for menopausal women. The foals were a byproduct. They were humanely destroyed.

At the track, Richard had seen many crippled Thoroughbred mares, finished as racehorses. He offered to take them for free and ended up with 10 well-made mares to send to Canada. The arrangement was made that we could pick the foals we wanted at three months old, and pick them up at five months of age. This did not work out for two reasons. One, Thoroughbred mares do not give the same quantity of urine that a draft mare does. Two, the fly and mosquito population in Canada is insufferable to a Thoroughbred mare in the field. As a result, they died or walked incessantly in misery.

Richard decided to find Thoroughbred stallions in the same category and send them. I met Dorothy Morkis (then Sarkis), whose father had lots of racehorses and two stallions to give! They were both Argentine bred, known to be hardy. Richard found one other and went off to deliver them to Ontario. He instructed the farmers in their care, asking them not to put the stallions out during the day in the fly season. This worked out and we took about 20 foals a year!

My wonderful Barnabus, who competed at the high level in both dressage and jumping, was a result of this program. As was Cousin Rufus, who did the Newport Derby with me. Lots of good competitors came from this source. We learned to judge the very young foals. We ended up with some wonderful amateur horses, especially from Percheron mares crossed with Thoroughbred stallions.

In the end, crossing the border with 20 foals at this age became too difficult at the customs inspection. On the last trip, Richard was refused and sent back to Canada. The law was to inspect each animal at the border, but there was no pen into which one could unload. The local vet refused, wisely, to get into the body of the truck with 20 wild foals. Richard found a small alternative road and arrived home. But he never went back.

The source was finished and an era ended. We had a final festive yearly sale of foals which the public loved. We bid farewell to the PMU program.

RIDING LESSON

There is a story about the renowned painter and sculptor Michelangelo that relates very well to horse training. As a young man, Michelangelo had very little money, like many artists. He had envisioned a statue, but to buy the piece of marble that he needed would take almost all of his reserves. He decided to risk it all and he bought the marble. It should be known that if you make the first strike in the wrong way, a piece of marble can crumble into a thousand pieces at your feet. Michelangelo stood for three weeks in front of his marble, afraid to make the first move. In time he did, and the result was the very famous *David* that is recognized as one of the most important contributions made to the world by this artist.

Standing in front of a new horse that is young, recently acquired, or to be retrained, a rider is often in the same position as Michelangelo. Where to begin? What comes first?

The key to a horse is his neck; it is the gateway to all that follows. A wrong move or a wrong education at the beginning will cost a lot in the future. One needs to know the function of the neck in order to proceed with logic. The horse uses his neck for balance. The rider uses the neck as a connection with the totality of the horse behind that point. Riding the horse with the longest neck possible, and arranging the neck/shoulder attachment at the height which corresponds with the movement demanded, is the objective. Simple, yes. Easy, no.

The neck should be long because it is what the horse uses to balance himself. When you shorten it, you take away his ability to balance himself and are obliged to create the balance artificially. Good balance is easier found by riding forward with a long neck than by riding backward with a

A STORY ABOUT MICHELANGELO

short neck. This is exemplified by French rider Eric Navet, amongst others. De Nemethy used to say, *"Imagine that your reins are sticks, and push the head of your horse forward."* A good rule is to educate the horse to make a descent of the neck on command before you begin to ride on contact. In that way, you are prepared to lengthen the neck if it becomes too short.

The neck can be long and low. The neck of a racehorse is attached low on the shoulder as running downhill is faster than running uphill. For jumping or dressage, the neck should be set more toward the top of the shoulder than in front of the shoulder. The horse must allow the rider to best position his neck for the maximum freedom of the shoulder and the ease of movement that follows.

My cowboy friend, Frank Barnett, explains this way: *"On a young uneducated horse, we should expect them to be on their shoulder and we will use that to our advantage when establishing forward movement. As they progress, we will be more involved with balancing the forehand so that they will weigh the same on both ends."*

"Forward riding in an uphill balance" is an important part of the method of Henri Prudent. Henri is mostly interested in high level show jumping, but having also an event background, he, like many jumping riders, uses dressage principles to form horses in all disciplines.

There are some good rules to follow in all classical riding:

- Open a horse before you close him.
- Think before you close him.
- Close him by riding forward and up.

A sure method of knowing if the neck is poorly positioned is that the rein aids cause the neck to shorten, or cause the neck to invert. Of course, the ideal is to buy horses whose necks are attached toward the top of the shoulder, never near the bottom, unless you wish to win a race. However, the rider can choose where to best position the neck to liberate the shoulder if the horse follows the rein. Then, the rider must take the time to do so before asking for the movement or jump to follow.

It goes without saying that the horse is best served by being laterally soft in his neck as well as by being perfectly arranged on his shoulder. However, the positioning of his neck on the shoulder is more important than the suppleness in the immediate moment. As such, the neck and shoulder are the gateways to the horse.

Communication with the hind legs is only possible through a well-formed neck and shoulder. Lacking that, one can be blocked here from all future work. The basic and first work must be done well on a horse as well as on a piece of marble.

CHAPTER SIX
INTRODUCTION TO DRESSAGE

Our friendship with Dorothy (Dottie) Morkis and her friend, Cindy Biladeau (later Mikolka), was leading to further exploration in the discipline of dressage. Dottie was riding a Thoroughbred named Roger, who had raced for her father. Roger didn't know a lot but he was an extravagant mover. Dottie was tall and thin and sat beautifully. The presentation had only one flaw: Roger had a huge tongue and it hung out of his mouth, usually to the right. Dottie tried to ride in a way that hid this but it was pretty visible.

Cindy was already immersed in the study of dressage, being a student of Henry van Schaik in Vermont. She had a beautiful seat and competed in the discipline. We three were learning as much as we could, me by reading and riding a lot, Cindy by spending a lot of time in Vermont, and Dottie by riding her Thoroughbred as well as she could. In the end, Cindy married Karl Mikolka, who was the third rider under Podhajsky at the Spanish Riding School (SRS). She became a top rider and coach at the Grand Prix level.

Dottie, with the help of Ernst Bachinger, also from the SRS, bought a wonderful gray horse, Monaco. They were fifth individually and won a bronze medal with the team at the 1976 Montreal Olympics. I carried on with my studies with Karl Mikolka, who trained his riders at Friars Gate Farm for five years, and then with Reiner Klimke in Münster, Germany. All three of us girls went a long way in our passion for dressage from those modest beginnings!

It was the tour of the Spanish Riding School that changed our lives. In 1974, Podhajsky decided to take the SRS on a tour of the United States.

Dottie and Cindy were free to travel and they followed the show. They met the riders and memorized the music. They were dressage groupies! Richard and I were equally enthralled, but we had a huge school, training center, and boarding facility that required our presence. So we only went to the presentation in Boston and met the riders there. After the show, we invited them out to see our farm.

Their reaction was immediate and not unique. The riders were amazed at the quality of our lives. We had two cars. We had heat in our house. We had money to compete or go to restaurants as we chose. And, in their eyes, we were not top level. In Vienna, Karl had only ever owned a small Volkswagen, there was no heat in the palace where they lived, and their salaries were comparable to Post Office salaries. Many of the riders began to look for better opportunities. To the great loss of the SRS, during their tour, they had witnessed the difference in their lives and ours. Years later, Podhajsky was heard saying that he would never repeat the tour as he lost his best riders because of it.

After Karl Mikolka married Cindy, they accepted a position in Brazil to train the Brazilian dressage team. When this position became untenable due to the instability of the government there, they returned to the USA. Richard and I offered them the use of Friars Gate Farm as a base for their training. And thus, my formal training began! It was five years of magic at our school. Cindy was our example and Karl was a constant source of technique and information. Soon we had ponies doing the piaffe and one that did the capriole, as Karl was an expert in airs above the ground. He rode my horses and I rode some of his to help make this an exchange. In the beginning, he was sent horses of lower quality than I was riding. This changed as he trained them all to do the higher level movements.

Karl taught the Weyrother method of dressage. It is only one of the methods taught at the SRS, but it was a method that he loved and he was generous in his explications of it. I had never read of this method and it fascinated me. The horses learned it very easily and the precision appealed to me. Karl explained that he was a taught rider, not a natural rider. The Weyrother method is a very factual method and can be learned by any horse or rider. Talent, in Karl's opinion, would facilitate learning, but education was more important than talent. At the time, I could not find a book that was written on the method. Karl told me that it must be passed down from master to student. I was honored to be one of his students. Recently, I learned that the book explaining the Weyrother method was locked in the library at the SRS during the reign of Podhajsky. When Colonel Hans Handler took over after the decease of this illustrious leader, he unlocked the library for all riders to use.

There were some small difficulties with the ponies who learned to do the airs above the ground. The dark brown pony who did the capriole was first trained in hand. Karl would put the pony into the piaffe until the moment seemed right and then gave a touch of the whip to incite the capriole. Soon after, little Richie Kelly, who later became a race jockey of some note, was placed in the saddle without stirrups to ride the movement, always in hand.

The problem became apparent when the pony was ridden in the Under Saddle class in the Pony Hunter division. If he was placed, Richie was obliged to ride to the ringmaster, who then took the pony by the bridle in order to hand the ribbon to Richie. To the pony, this was too similar to the way he was asked to do the capriole. He would immediately produce a spectacular leap, frightening all the local ringmasters! He was a crowd favorite! Richie became a star and the local spectators always came to watch the Under Saddle phase, in hopes that the pony would be called out. However, I could not sell or lease this pony, as most parents could not see this as an opportunity to learn. His capriole was of excellent quality.

At the time, we had a big group of school horses. Karl decided to use some of them as possible horses for the levade and piaffe in hand in order to help with training riders. Oliver was one of these horses. He was a less than perfect school horse because he could not canter. He was frightened of speed and also of his own shadow. Years later, I realized that he may have been vision-impaired. He did a lovely levade and was elevated to the yearly exhibition. Karl believed, and proved, that every horse should have a life.

The exhibition was presented every April at Friars Gate. It was a duplicate of the Sunday Performance at the SRS. There were some small changes in the quadrille, as we never had eight horses to finish in passage. One of the hardest parts of the quadrille was that the horses were required to do 14 steps at the canter across the short end of the ring in order to stay in the right place. All the pirouettes had to be at the same speed. It was very tricky riding. The entire performance was done by children, students, and horses from the farm. All my jumpers were used. Of course, it was directed by Karl. The Pas de Deux was always Richard and the smallest rider on a tiny pony. One year, this was Mary Anne McInnis on a pony that was 11.2 hands. At the very end, there was a good jumping demonstration, which was good for the morale of everyone after a month of hard work and rehearsals. There was always a huge crowd in the grandstand, which was made of hay bales. Every year was an adventure, and it made our school.

One of my dreams was to find a way to go to Germany and see the dressage competitions. This dream came true because of the Boris Terfloth family from Montreal, Canada. At the 1976 Montreal Olympics, the riders were housed in private homes. The Terfloth family invited Reiner Klimke to stay at their home during the competition. At the time, I was training young Mark Terfloth, who was a student at Milton Academy near Boston. I was also riding a horse for the family, Troubadour, who was one of the finest young jumpers I had ever ridden. When Marc finished his studies and left for university, the Terfloths gave me his horse, Travel Along, who was an intermediate jumper. They also asked me what they could do to help me in my career. I replied that I would love to go to Germany to watch dressage competitions.

They immediately contacted Reiner, who invited me to his stable to watch. Richard agreed that I should leave Friars Gate in his hands and take this opportunity to ride in Germany. Having just finished the Wellington Circuit, my horses needed rest, and I went off to Münster, Germany. Karl advised me to show up at the stable in riding clothes and with a long, warm coat. It was the best advice!

Reiner was a practicing lawyer. He only rode during lunchtime and later after office hours. He could ride two or three during lunch and called to have the first horse prepared when he left the office. It was the same procedure in the evening, at about 7:30 p.m. He did not like to ride until the horses had made at least 25 descents of the head. In this, I was an expert, due to Karl's insistence on the same warm-up. I could make any horse put his head very low and remain connected. It gave me an advantage in warming up Reiner's horses.

When I first visited Reiner in Münster, he explained that one of the most important goals in training a high level dressage horse is to arrive at the Grand Prix level without ruining the youthful exuberance of the horse. Dressage training can never be a way to dominate a horse. It is a way to educate and condition a horse. In this spirit, dressage is wonderful for jumping horses because the horse does not lose his own initiative.

Reiner worked his horses in plain snaffles, mostly with no spurs or whips. The full bridle was used at home on Sundays, on the horses that were at the level required to use it. Even then, he warmed up in the snaffle and changed to the full bridle when the horse was warmed up. He did the same at competitions, changing bridles before entering the ring.

He criticized the German system of that time. He deplored the heavy, driving seat in fashion at the time. He had a strong but light position on the horse. I was amazed that even the strongest horse could not move him from his seat if he did not want to be moved. He never accepted the idea of sitting back, sitting heavily, or driving with his seat. This I appreciated very much and it was exactly as I had been advised by Karl.

Reiner let me ride his horses. He explained that he did not teach, but I could learn by riding and by watching. Ahlerich was a five-year-old at the time, and very hot. Reiner knew that the horse had a huge future, but he was lame due to a splint. He told me to ride the horse while he was at his law practice so that he did not have to see the horse in a lame condition. Ahlerich did not think that he was lame. He was explosive! Reiner told me to be very careful that the horse did not hurt himself, but I was more concerned with myself! Later, this horse went on to become the World Champion. During his demonstration in New York, he won the hearts of everyone who saw it. He still had his joie de vivre!

After several weeks, one evening, Reiner asked me what method it was that I rode. He had watched me riding and he was curious. I told him that I had learned the Weyrother method from a rider of the SRS. He was aghast. He took a step backward, saying that the method was brutal and that I should not use it on his horses. Dismayed, I agreed, but I knew very little else to use at the level I was riding on his horses. I was given one of Reiner's wife Ruth's wonderful horses, Sekur, to ride occasionally. I found this method the best for him. So I continued but in disguise.

After a month, again in the evening, he told me that he knew that I was still using this method. I paled, but as I began to explain, he stopped me.

"Wait," he said, *"I have seen that the method is not severe as you ride it. The method is less important than the manner of the rider, and with you, it is fine. You can continue."* He was very open-minded and cared only for the spirit of his horses. Reiner was an Olympic gold medalist six times. His principle of retaining the spirit and joie de vivre of a top-level horse is the epitome of the discipline. His and Ruth's generosity in letting me ride all of those horses and confiding in me his underlying strategies enriched my life.

My formal training in dressage consisted of the time spent with Karl Mikolka and Reiner Klimke. Since then, I have never stopped learning from my horses, from books, and from my great friends, like Jack Le Goff. Jack never hesitated to have discussions with me. He was always patient enough to listen to all my discoveries and experiments before laying a hand on my shoulder and telling me his opinion. He was an exceptional horseman who trained the U.S. event team to many medals and championships in his long tenure in America.

Dressage was my passion. I enjoyed both the French method of my good friend Jack Le Goff and the Weyrother method taught to me by Karl Mikolka. I loved the details and precision of these methods. I have relied upon these principles of dressage to train and condition show jumpers all my life.

RIDING LESSON

One of the most important types of stretching work for a horse is the "long and low" work that one does at the beginning and end of every session. It is vastly misunderstood. It is worth the time to learn what the important details of the work are and how to do it correctly, because, done incorrectly, it can go exactly in the wrong direction, accomplishing more bad than good.

The silhouette that is desired is very precise, in that no matter to which degree the horse succeeds in lowering his neck, the throatlatch must be open. That is another way of saying that the nose of the horse must be in front of the vertical. The connection between the head and the neck of the horse will give the impression of being oval if this work has been done correctly, or more the impression of forming an "A" if the work has been done wrong. The upper third of the neck is no less important than the other two parts of the neck.

More important than the silhouette of the neck or the degree of the lowering of the neck during stretching is the fact that the horse must exert some small pressure on the rein as he stretches. Without this small pressure, the work is not correct. A good way to understand this is with this example: A human can touch his toes as a stretching exercise before work by simply letting his hands fall to the lowest level possible; or, he can push with a small pressure downwards against his toes. The effect on the spine is completely different and can be felt immediately. Without the push downwards, the stretching has much less benefit.

All artificial reins, like the gogue, chambon, drawrein, and Pessoa, that are used to create a silhouette eliminate the possibility of this second

IT ALL BEGINS WITH STRETCHING

and most important phase of the descent of the neck. The proof that the work has been done correctly is the shape of the neck while the horse is standing in a normal position. The connection between the head and the neck should give an oval impression, the under-neck muscle should be less developed than the top line, and there should be no hollow or hole just in front of the shoulder. The neck of the horse is a mirror of his back. One can change the neck with correct work in about a month, and the back will follow in the same way in two or three months, depending on its condition at the beginning. Working the horse in the long and low position is important in the development of flexibility.

There are two kinds of flexibility in the horse: lateral and longitudinal. One contributes to the other, but the first is always lateral, and it is this lateral bending work that triggers the good lengthening of the neck. Anyone can do this in five minutes with proper instruction. The lengthening produced in this way will be correct in that the horse will push gently on the reins in his lowest position. The artificial lengthening created by one of the artificial auxiliary reins listed above produces no lateral flexibility. Because of that, the work produces very little lasting benefit.

As easy as it is to do the correct lengthening, there really is no excuse to do it incorrectly. It is not because our riders are lazy that this is not being done, it is because our instructors are not motivated to go through this type of lengthy discourse over and over to make the concept understandable. I submit this short discourse as a way forward in the understanding of lateral bending being the contributing factor in the correct stretching of the neck.

CHAPTER SEVEN
INTO THE CHASE

Fox hunting has always been another passion of mine. I love horses and I love hounds. I wanted to share that part of the horse sport with my students. We had no opportunity to hunt at Friars Gate Farm, but I arranged to take groups of my equitation riders to hunt the challenging country in Ireland. When doing so, I was obliged to lie. Upon contacting the Lamb family for my first hunting trip, I was informed that all juniors were to have been previously out with hounds and be familiar with the hunting protocol. *"No ring riders!"* I was told.

I selected my group of good riders who could happily masquerade as veteran fox hunters. I decided to take my best 12-year-old riders who were brave, lacking in inhibitions, and ready for this test. We practiced the hunting terms in the indoor: "Hold hard! Tally ho!" I did suggest they be cautious about the latter, and let an older rider have that honor: *"Ware hound!" "Ware whip!"* We also practiced greeting and thanking the Master, turning the heads of our horses toward the hounds, and never passing a member of the staff. The only thing for which I could not prepare for were the ditches around Tipperary!

We set off for Ireland during Thanksgiving school break, a tradition that I would follow for 10 years. I had selected Mary Anne McInnis, Jan O'Donnell, Gardner Powell, Emily Roberts, and Tasia Watson as my accomplished fox hunters, although they were really equitation or hunter riders at the time. Mary Anne was later one of my best equitation riders, winning the Zone One final three times in a row. Gardner Powell, now instrumental in the intercollegiate program, was successful in all three divisions for juniors. As a group, they were highly qualified to ride any type of horse. They were prepared for the masquerade. Jan O'Donnell was a last-minute add. She was tired of university and in a low mood. She needed an adventure.

As we arrived at the hunt, we greeted the Master, found our place politely at the rear, and waited for the hounds to find the line of a fox. They found one! Instantly, the Field split into four groups, each galloping wildly off in separate directions! *"Follow me!"* yelled a man I didn't know. *"I know this fox! He will go this way!"* I followed him instead of the hounds, which was not my understanding of the hunt etiquette, but we were in Ireland!

When we arrived at the first big ditch, Mary Anne gasped, *"How do I stay on!?"* She is a meticulous and detailed rider who is always well-prepared. I told her to use the martingale strap and went in front. We met again in about 10 minutes and she held up the broken martingale as she galloped past me with a big grin.

A hireling went lame and as the rider was an amateur, I gave him my horse and led the lame one back to the truck. On my way, I stood aside to let the Master pass at full gallop, followed by one remaining rider: Gardner Powell. On a pony! As the Master passed me, he gave me a thumbs up toward Gardner, who had a big smile and plenty of mud on her face. I was congratulated for bringing seasoned juniors to hunt. The kids were gleeful that we had put one over on the Irish!

The next day, on Sunday, we went out with a foot pack. Jan outsmarted us all, having read that the red fox runs in a circle. She stayed on top of a bank, while we climbed down into the water, ran across the field, repeated several banks, and ended up beside Jan. She had never moved. My kids were smart alecks.

Jan and I went to the dance on the last night of our visit, and I asked the younger kids to pack up for our departure the next morning. When we came home late, the luggage was in the front hall. Suddenly, I realized that one of the bigger bags was moving. We quickly opened the bag and found little Emily packed into a bag! I am sure, but have no proof, that Tasia and Gardner were responsible. Emily was psychologically unscathed.

For the next nine years, every year I took students and friends to Ireland to hunt with me. Scarteen became my Irish base and Thady and Anne Ryan my good friends. I learned most of what I know about hounds from Thady. There were many adventures in the country surrounding Knocklong.

On one trip, I arrived to find Thady wearing a collar around a broken neck. He explained that I would be required to hunt a horse that he was trying as a replacement for his aging favorite. He was to follow in the truck to see how the horse got on in that country. I flew over the big iron gate and never paused in front of the fearful ditches. But he was a flat-out runaway! How I finished the day, I don't know, but I advised him not to buy the horse. His eyes were shining as he laughingly told me that the horse would never again be in the Field. He would be out in front as the Master! He bought the horse immediately.

On one trip, I had convinced Lellie Ward, an American event rider and experienced jockey, to accompany me. When we arrived, Thady took us aside and begged us, *"Please, none of your antics!"* A famous journalist was staying at Scarteen to write an article about the Black and Tan Hounds, which had been in the Ryan family for generations. The journalist would also enjoy a day out with Scarteen. It also came out that the lovely wife of the journalist was afraid of flying things.

The drapes in the dining room were old. They had been there for generations of the Ryan family. I knew that they had to be handled carefully as they were heavily infested with Monarch butterflies. Anne pulled the drapes for dinner. So when Anne came to the drawing room to invite us to the table, I leaped up and announced, *"I will get the drapes!"*

"NO! NO!" cried Thady, knowing what I was going to do. Too late. I ran across the hall and whipped the drapes sharply across the window. A huge flock of butterflies took flight across the dining room just as the illustrious couple entered. The journalist's wife fled. Thady shook his finger at me before following her back to the salon to convince her that they would not fly during dinner.

The following day, after a long check on the hill overlooking the little town of Hospital, Lellie and I were having a conversation with the journalist while waiting for the hounds to speak. His horse appeared restless, turning about and pawing. Suddenly, he went down into the mud to roll and the celebrity was down in the mud with him! Aghast, he stumbled to his feet, covered in mud, and exclaimed, *"I never thought he would go down!"* Lellie replied, in a bright and cheery voice, for all to hear, *"That's what they said on the Titanic!"* Amid roars of laughter, the red-faced journalist took the back of the Field as hounds found a scent, and we were off. Thady was apprehensive about the ensuing article, but I assume it came out okay.

The hunting world is full of stories of adventure at Scarteen, from the midnight rat hunts in long skirts after dinner with Anne's terriers in the hayloft to the race for the one bathtub after the hunt. Anne turned the heat on for the hot water when the cars came into the yard after the hunt. This was because the routine stop at the pub could take more or less time than estimated. It could take 20 minutes to get enough hot water for a bath, but everyone tried to get there first.

One day, Thady had come home directly, never stopping at the pub, to repair some roof tiles. To get onto the roof, one climbed up a folding ladder out the trap door over the tub in the bathroom. Thady climbed up, folded the ladder, closed the trap behind him, and went to work. Gail Wofford, the wife of Jimmy Wofford, a medal winner for the U.S. event team and president of the US federation, won the race for the bathtub, undressed, and got into the tub to wait for hot water. Imagine the shocked expressions when Thady opened the trap to climb down from the roof! I never heard exactly how this ended, but dinner was eaten that evening in the usual spirit.

Over the years, I convinced many skeptics to come with me on my yearly hunting adventure. Margaret Lee, head of the Foxcroft Riding Department, broke her collarbone on the first hunt and happily chatted in the pubs as a spectator for the rest of her trip. Holly Caristo fell after a huge ditch and bank, and I was unable to stop my horse, so we jumped the ditch—and Holly! I had a hard time justifying that to my friend Ralph Caristo upon our return. Muffy Seaton, an international driving competitor, was scared to hunt a horse she had never ridden, so I took the group to Galway, where one jumps only walls and no ditches. There, I told her to follow me closely. After jumping four walls, she shot past me laughing. *"This is a gas!"* she cried. I did not see her again until we met at the pub later.

When Thady decided to retire and hand the horn to his son Chris, Anne wisely decided that they should move back to her home in New Zealand. Most of the family had already emigrated, and it would give Chris and his wife Sue the space to develop Scarteen as they wished. They have done a wonderful job with the big old house and the kennels. I had a much longer trip to make to visit my friends on the South Island of New Zealand, but I could see that it was a good life for them both.

I only hunted in England once. I was hired to hunt a horse with the Pytchley Hunt, to try him for a friend as a possible purchase for hunting in Virginia. When I arrived, I was pleased to be dressed in my best hunting clothes as this was not Ireland! There were many out in the Field from London and many pink coats. When they threw me up onto my horse, I was told to force my way to the front at the very beginning at the risk of never seeing hounds all day if I didn't. *"These Londoners are thrusters,"* I was told.

We were all lined up, side by side, on top of a huge hill, waiting for the slightest whimper of a hound to indicate a scent. Horses were piaffing, leaping, and spinning in anticipation of what was to come: a race to the first coop at the bottom of that hill. I heard a hound! So did everyone else! We were off at a gallop, neck and neck. There were 100 in the field, but 20 of us were in the first flight. All 20 of us were contesting the same coop at the bottom, which could accommodate two or three horses at a time. I raced for the left-hand side of the coop, and I was slightly faster than the Londoner on my left. He was riding a lovely tall gray hireling and was impeccably dressed in a top hat and all. He stubbornly refused to yield to my victory and ended up jumping the wire fence to the left of the coop. What a folly! On the other side of that wire fence was a liquid slurry used to store manure in liquid form. He made a huge splash and I never saw him again, as I gleefully galloped on to my deserved view of the hounds. At the end of the day, I learned that he had returned to the truck immediately and left in his rented car in a muddy and smelly condition.

We bought the horse I tried! He went back to a more civil atmosphere in Virginia where thrusters are to be disdained.

RIDING LESSON

Possibly one of the most important physical qualities of a fine rider is balance. The balance of a rider on a horse is especially important, and difficult because the horse is moving. A rider who stays precisely over the center of balance of his horse makes himself easy to carry. A rider who can discreetly shift his balance before the horse moves can influence the horse with no rein or leg aid.

Balance cannot be taught. One is born with the sensitivity, agility, and suppleness that makes it possible. However, it can be understood. To understand the balance of a rider who makes himself easy and light to carry, one needs to understand the balance of the horse in moving. The horse must shift his balance each time he accelerates, slows down, turns, or jumps. The degree to which he changes his balance depends on the degree of the movement. Once the horse is in motion, unchanging and steady, a rider can stay in his place, like a skier on a smooth downhill slope. It is only during transitions, turns, and jumping efforts that the real rider becomes apparent. Here are a few examples of this.

The turning horse lowers his inside hip and shoulder to facilitate the turn. The rider should remain parallel to his horse, with more weight on the inside stirrup than the outside, to the same degree as his horse. The huge modern misunderstanding, caused by the effect of the centrifugal force, is that the rider puts all his weight on the outside stirrup. This makes the turn difficult for the horse and adds a step to the turn. To correct this tendency, many trainers suggest riding with no stirrups. Years ago, Victor Hugo Vidal encouraged riding with only one stirrup, the inner one, for a more sophisticated correction.

THE BALANCE OF THE RIDER

The center of balance of an accelerating horse, or a jumping one, is slightly in front of the withers. In order to help a horse in the acceleration, the rider needs to be over that center of balance. The huge modern misunderstanding caused by horses that are not trained to the leg is that the rider sits down behind the movement to accelerate. This makes the acceleration slower, coupled many times with a lowering of the back. The best and simplest correction for this error is Katie Prudent's command, *"As the horse speeds up, lighten your seat. As the horse slows down, sink into the saddle."* The horse must go forward from the leg if this correction is accepted.

The horse which finds himself a little close to the jump, must shift his weight to the rear at the takeoff. The rider needs to make the same small shift. The enormous problem, caused by an incomplete understanding of the use of the stirrup as an aid, is that the rider opens his shoulders and sits down. This makes the ensuing takeoff more difficult, exaggerates the movement of the rider to catch up with the jump, and can lower the back of the horse. The best solution for this is to increase the weight in the stirrup to shift the balance slightly backward without interfering with the jump. Gustav Steinbrecht's book, *The Gymnasium of the Horse*, on the use of the stirrup, and, more recently, Karl Mikolka's teachings on the same subject, should be required reading for all riders in the jumping disciplines.

The level of riding in all disciplines has evolved over the past few decades to an ever higher standard. The untrained young rider who only rides by instinct is finding it impossible to keep his place. Instinct must be in a balance with education. Many times the latter is more important than the former. The riders who are forming the future of our sport are never ending in the search for more answers and more ideas. It is a thrilling time.

CHAPTER EIGHT
SUMMER CAMP ERA

Friars Gate Farm had grown by the seventies, and there were over 100 horses in training on those 15 acres that were originally a woodlot. It was becoming increasingly difficult for me to leave my students every summer in order to operate the summer stable, Dennis Riding School, on Cape Cod. A solution was found in the form of Friars Gate Camp, which was a camp of my own for serious young riders aged 9 to 14, and also for riders who wanted a total horse immersion summer and who were suggested to me by other professionals. The camp was located on the same property as Dennis Riding School. It was agreed that I would run the camp, while Richard would run the public riding school.

Along with three hours of mounted instruction each day, there were stable management classes, routine barn work, and equine arts and crafts. One learned to make cottons to use under bandages, construct a hay bag using twine, fashion earplugs to match the color of each horse, and so forth. One year, the campers built a barn with Richard. The boys all learned to drive the tractor. We had cross-country races on the trails and on the power line, frightening most local riders away forever. Richard took everyone to the local sandpit on horses to teach them to slide all the way to the bottom. We swam the horses in our pond as often as possible. Being a Friars Gate Camp survivor became a mark of pride.

We showed at local shows with all the campers and tried to secure three-year-olds so that the campers could start them under saddle. Most campers came with their own horse but we supplied the young horses. I believe in starting young horses as a group whenever possible. Horses are herd animals, and 10 three-year-olds can be easily trained to carry riders as they work around a small ring with the trainer in the middle to direct them. It is only when a horse is removed from the herd and then saddled and ridden that the difficulties arise.

I cooked, drove the horse van, taught, and supervised, while riding my own horses before breakfast and after supper. It was a big group at meals with both campers and the workers who ran the Dennis Riding School with Richard. These workers were generally graduate campers. Campers were between 7 and 14 years old. Workers were from 15-year-olds to young adults. I was cooking for eighteen people!

Richard was intrigued with the food procurement for this crowd. He was a constant source of energy in finding economic ways of feeding the camp. One day, he asked me, in a sly manner I had come to know, "Which is the meat you need the most to feed everyone during the summer?" I thought about that for a moment and answered, "Hamburger! I make meatloaf, meatballs, and hamburgers." He smiled, and left. Later, he came back to announce that a local cattle breeder had retired and had offered his old herd bull to Richard at a very cheap price. Richard bought the bull and sent him to be made into hamburger.

The butcher called to say that he was taking more time with this order as the meat was so tough that it had to be ground three times. Later, he called again to ask if he could add some fat to the product as the meat did not cook well at all. In the end, I made hamburgers and meatloaf that necessitated a fork and knife to eat them. The campers thought it was a great story!

There were rare instances when the campers and workers were not happy with Richard's Food Procurement Project. One of these times was when Richard found that dented and unlabeled cans could be picked up free from the rear of the supermarket every Wednesday. Richard claimed that he could tell the contents of a can by shaking the can and listening carefully. He tried to instruct the group in this skill and they spent hours on the porch after dinner working at it. However, they drew the line at the cans of tuna, because they could not be distinguished from the cans of cat food. The second time they drew the line was the episode of survival crackers. The historic center of Boston was being redeveloped at this time. The city needed places to dump clean rubble, cobblestones, cement pilings, and steel rods. Since our farm desperately needed fill to raise the back field,

Richard made a deal: the rubble would be dumped and spread on our back acres. We ended up with an all-weather dirt-covered field for the grass arena. Richard made regular trips to Boston to see what was coming. On one of these trips, he discovered the bomb shelter in the basement of the Telephone Building. It was fully stocked with dried food for three months. Survival crackers, as we came to know them, were part of the stock.

Richard returned happily with many tins of these crackers. He announced that from now on, we would serve crackers and cheese before dinner. He confided in me that a survival cracker swells in the stomach and can equal a day's needs nutritionally. At first, the group was very happy with this improved appetizer course. But after three days, little Richie Kelly was the first to suspect something amiss with the crackers. "Something fishy", is how he put it. The campers all approached Richard and he confessed. There was nothing Richard could do that would ever lessen his popularity with those kids. They loved his antics.

I had some wonderful riders at that camp, such as Karen O'Connor (then Lende), who became a top event rider in the country for many years, and Ed Marcy, who stayed on to run the riding school with Richard. Later, Ed moved to California and continued his career as a rider and teacher. Many future professional and top level amateur riders were part of the double program of camp and riding school. They were pretty mischievous. They painted the town water tower one night! It was hard work but it was fun. Gardner Powell was unequaled in her imaginative games of short sheeting and other pranks.

I also tried to instill good ethics in the camp. It was a goal for each camper to do something nice, like a favor, for another camper or worker every day without being found out. Years later, Joe Fargis told me that one of my ex-campers rode with Joe and told him about that. He told me that he never forgot what a good impression it had made on that student. The camp was a total immersion experience: very hard but also rewarding to everyone because of the progress. The idea of total dedication to horses while learning proved so successful that it led me to start to dream of my working student program, with older riders in their late teens or early 20s, later on.

RIDING LESSON

To be at the top of any sport one needs to be very talented. Talent, like feeling, cannot be taught. One is born with talent and one develops feeling over time as a result of a sensitive nature. In the earlier days of our sport, a rider with great talent could rise to the top, even with very little formal education. The equestrian sport, in every discipline, has evolved to the point where formal education, or method-in-training, has taken on almost equal importance to talent as a characteristic of a top rider. In the show jumping discipline, this evolution has been produced by the sophistication of the course designers, and the shortened time allowed to complete the course. The competition at the high level has become highly technical, and a solid education and method have become a prerequisite for both rider and horse.

There are many methods of training horses, each of which has its own characteristics and form. In order to learn a method, one must be willing to spend at least a year in complete immersion in that method. Even though it is an advantage to know several methods, it is impossible to learn more than one at a time. When learning languages, one can study Spanish, French, and English during the same year, but this cannot be considered a total immersion. In learning an art, as in learning to train horses, total immersion is by far the fastest road to competence. The unhappy realization by many riders, having mixed parts of many methods into a confusing melange that does not work for the majority of horses or students, is that total immersion in one method is the fastest road to competence.

A horse trained and ridden by a talented and inventive rider can many times be impossible to ride by the succeeding rider. A horse trained

TALENT AND METHOD

by a talented and methodical rider can easily be ridden at the same level by other riders who are qualified to do so. An example of this is Beezie Madden and Cortes C, who was successfully ridden by Beezie and all three other finalists at the 2014 World Equestrian Games in Caen, France. Beezie was once a protégé of Katie Prudent, who is adamant that one year of total immersion was the way to learn a method. The true test of the methodical trainer is the performance of his horse with the next rider. Another test is the number of horses with which that trainer or rider arrives at the high level. On the other hand, it is not a positive remark to say that, *"No one else can follow his ride."*

To learn a method takes a year of total immersion. Clinics, the occasional lesson, and videos cannot take the place of all-day, constant exposure to a method. Time invested will always produce results. Classical methods, like the Caprilli method, Weyrother method, De Nemethy method, French method, and American method, are all systematic, progressive, and rich in detail and tradition. Learning to ride, and later to train and to coach, is the same as learning to become a doctor, in that one must go to school. No one wants a talented surgeon who never went to med school.

Those students who suffer the one-year immersion test will invariably repeat it by learning a second method, having found the enormous benefit of the first effort. Those students are the future of our sport and become the trainers of the future. The many very talented riders who choose to ride by instinct and feeling alone may enjoy huge individual accomplishments, but contribute less to the equestrian world in the larger picture. As our sport evolves, the combination of talent with method becomes imperative as a way to succeed in a regular fashion with many horses on many continents.

In forming young horses in a methodical way, one can produce confident, sound, and technically correct horses for a long future in the sport. Every horse is different. The talent and feeling of a rider is what allows him to use the same method on many horses, adjusted in terms of the personality and physical state of each horse.

A method used with no feeling can rapidly become drilling or repetitive, and thereby spirit breaking. Reiner Klimke often said that the challenge of training a Grand Prix dressage horse was not to teach the movements, but to do so without destroying the character of a young horse. And so, the instinct and finesse of the rider are what makes the method successful.

In today's world, with competition becoming more and more sophisticated and at higher levels every year, to be at the top a rider must have great talent and a solid education in at least one method. Talent alone is not enough, and the time invested in learning is always well repaid over the years that follow.

CHAPTER NINE
FRIARS GATE FARM

Returning to Friars Gate Farm in the fall was a complete change for me because I was no longer the cook. The riding and training of over 100 horses, with no paddock available, was a massive organization. Every night, "The Day Sheet" was prepared with the activity for each horse. All serious students rode two horses after school. There was a riding school of non-owners that used almost 20 horses and ponies a day. There were owners who rode their own horses. There were the 17 horses in Karl and Cindy's dressage school.

Every day, I began early enough to ride 14 horses and give a required staff lesson before the children arrived from school at 2:30 p.m. All staff were required to take part in one lesson a day as a measure of solidarity and benefit for all. Then, lessons began and lasted until 6 p.m. when the parents picked everyone up for dinner.

Every Saturday evening, we built the course for the next week's work. On Sunday, the students all jumped their horses over this course. After they had ridden their own horses, they were allowed to continue to jump all day on the school horses or ponies until every horse in the program had been jumped. This was free training and I did it gladly because it improved my riders so much to ride all those horses.

On Mondays, we turned all the horses out at liberty in groups of 20 in the indoor, with their sheets or blankets on. This prevented injury while they had an opportunity to buck and play. This activity was not shared by dressage horses. If you missed school for some reason, there was a game on Mondays. The horses were let into the indoor, one by one, through the sliding door from the attached shed row barn. A rider could pick a horse and get on him in the barn before being let loose with the herd. The last rider on a horse after the play was over was the winner of the day! It was hard to follow the action because of the dust as we did not water the ring on Mondays. Each rider that fell off would run out into the shed row barn, declaring his or her name as they fled. At the end, I would cry, *"Is anyone still on?"*

"Yes, ME!" cried a voice one Monday. *"Ritchie Kelly! I am here!"* But when he arrived at the door, I saw that he was riding Apple Dandy, and he had entered the ring on Cymbal. When I asked for an explanation, he admitted to having been thrown from the first, but he claimed to have landed on the second, never having touched the ground! It's no wonder he became such a good racing rider.

My idea of teaching riding is the same as my idea of training horses. The spirit is the secret of learning. Fun and adventure play a role in training. The poet, Charles Bukowski, was quoted as saying, *"When the spirit is dead, form is born."* He was complaining about the strict rules to be followed in writing a sonnet. His sonnet, not filling the criteria, had been rejected by the publishers. I believe that his sentiment can be applied to training horses and riders. Personal style, humor, imagination, and instinct must never be sacrificed for form. Real education and factual knowledge cannot be replaced as a basis, but there must be room left for spirit, adventure, and risk. A student that did not fit into the pattern never bothered me.

One day, a young boy of about 11 years came to speak to me as I was walking out of the ring. He looked at the ground so I had to listen carefully.

"Um," he began. *"Um, could you give me a lesson?"*

"Sure," I said. *"Have you ever ridden?"*

"Yep," was the reply, and nothing more.

"Well, do you have a horse or do you want to ride one of mine?"

"I have one. He is a palomino."

"Okay, well, does he have a Western saddle or English?"

"He can jump," was the reply.

"Oh! So you have jumps at home for him?"

"No, but I can jump my father's car."

Without asking for the make of the car, I invited the boy, Andy, to ride his palomino over the very next day. He had minimized this horse! He floated over the course, the boy in a loaned hard hat and work boots. When he finished, my mouth was open. I had to know where he got this horse. He told me that it was a gift from his uncle to get him started. We ended up at Madison Square Garden with this horse and his blonde kid rider. His uncle turned out to be the very well-known Dr. Howie Raven, a veterinarian for the Greenwich, Connecticut, area. Andy Wills was a misfit in dressage and systematic training. The horse never went in a frame, yet they jumped together brilliantly. He was a great rider.

To allow for the individual without disturbing the huge group of riders and horses training in such a small place, rules were set in place for all. Winters in New England are long and start early. With dressage horses and show jumpers sharing the indoor arena, I had to learn to build courses for the jumpers which left the center line and the diagonals free. All riders were well-versed in the riding rules. Riders following the center line or the diagonals have the right of way. Horses doing work in hand or on the long rein stay on the track, while others yield. Shoulder-in and renvers yield the track to oncoming traffic, while leg yielding and travers along the wall keep the track in that situation. One always enlarges the circle to enclose another rider who is in the path. Riders not working, at walk, ride off the path. One never overtakes another rider, but it is the responsibility of the rider that would be overtaken to cut off the corner of the ring to give priority to the better mover behind.

All of the European rules of riding indoors in groups are logical and to the benefit of the horse. In learning these rules, one is obliged to know where everyone is and what they are doing. This shows community spirit. Young riders and juniors are taught these riding rules in Europe just as children learn table manners at home. Knowing these manners is a comfort when one is at a new stable.

The exposure of the jumping riders to the training practices of the dressage riders was an extremely important part of their formation. Having a combined stable of two disciplines with two different professionals was not a problem, but a huge advantage to all involved. Karl took a big interest in my junior students and taught them things that they had never seen in dressage.

Most days, we also had spectators watching us work. The huge grandstand made of hay bales, originally used for the Exhibition in April, became a permanent fixture for spectators. This was welcomed by the parents as it was a warm place to watch the lessons.

RIDING LESSON

I think all of us like to train horses; that's why we began this. Horses are a lot of fun, and the joy of horses is that there are no two alike. When you're going toward the same goal with every horse and that's what you like to do with them, like show jump, field hunt, or dressage, you probably try to do that more or less the same way with every horse. But it isn't the same thing because every horse is slightly different and you need to be able to be flexible in the way you approach a horse. Your method must correspond with that horse's personality.

A lot of methods have been developed over the years. In fact, since the 1600s, there have been methods of training horses. Each method corresponds with a certain type of horse. A person who is educated in many of these classical methods can talk to or educate practically any horse he comes across in his whole life.

Whereas with a person who forms his own personal method, you might have heard him say, *"My method is a good method. Look, I trained three horses in a row now and every one of those horses goes really well. Now, I have this fourth horse and I can't do a thing with him. He doesn't respond to me, he doesn't want to learn, so I'm going to have to get tough with this horse and be a little stricter with him."* Actually, the problem is not the horse, and it isn't the rider either. It's the method.

If he was willing to show the flexibility of a really good trainer, he would change his method. Many riders do not know very many methods; they only know the one that they learned at the beginning. It takes a lot of methods to be a real horse trainer because you have to be able to change your method to suit the horse that you're training.

CHOOSING YOUR METHOD

Let me tell you a story about my father. At the end of World War II, he decided that he would take us kids to Germany to see evidence of what had been going on and to see the ravages of war. He wanted to go right away before they made a parking lot out of what was a national disgrace. He wanted to take us even though we were a little too young. So, we went off and we saw it all. He wanted us to see it because he wanted us to never repeat it.

One day, we stopped for lunch at a restaurant out in the country-side. My father didn't speak any German; he only spoke English. He said to the man, *"We would like a table for four for lunch, please."* It was a little too soon after the war and the Germans didn't really want you there; they didn't like Americans. The man said, *"Nicht verstehen,"* which means, *"I don't understand you."* My father repeated his question but louder. He said, *"We want a table for four for lunch."* The man said in the same tone of voice, *"Nicht verstehen."* My father wound up and yelled the same question at the man to see if he could make the man understand simply by volume. The man threw us out. So we left there and it was amazing that my father didn't start World War III.

I wonder if you see the parallel with that with some horse trainers. They canter across the diagonal and apply their aids for a flying change, and nothing happens. Or the horse either changes in front or not behind, he's disunited, or he doesn't know what to do. So the rider says, *"Alright, I'm going to try that again, but this time when I canter across that diagonal, I'm going to use my aids a little stronger."* And he does that, and nothing happens. The horse is disunited, he doesn't change at all, he gets all excited, and now the horse is a little nervous. So the guy gets off and he goes in the tack room and gets a stronger bit. He also gets a pair of spurs and a stick. He says, *"Now let me have him. Now I will canter across that diagonal and he's going to change his lead."*

This man is on his way to starting World War III because the horse still doesn't understand. The problem is not the aids, and it's not anything about that rider; it's that he's using a method that doesn't correspond with that horse. The horse doesn't understand it, and what happens then is that the horse loses his confidence in his handler because he doesn't understand him, and pretty soon, you need some expert to undo this baggage. They say in America, *"This horse is carrying a lot of baggage."* That means he's had a lot of bad handling. Bad handling is relative; riding the horse with the wrong method is bad handling. Many times this occurs from a lack of education on the part of the person who is riding or trying to train the horse.

Initially, I didn't know much about the German method. With all the reading I did when I was a kid, I had learned the Caprilli method. I had also learned the French method, and I knew that pretty well. We had De Némethy so we were exposed to the Hungarian method and Gordon Wright's method, with George Morris as the biggest protégé of that method. We knew some methods but I didn't understand the German method. So, I stopped everything and went to Germany. I rode for Reiner Klimke.

Reiner was a wonderful horseman. He didn't teach, but he said, *"You can ride my horses and you can watch me."*

I said, *"That's enough. I can do that."*

So I rode his horses and I watched him. After about a month, he said to me at a cocktail party, *"What is the system that you're riding because I don't know the system? I see what you're doing but I don't know the system."*

I said, *"It's the Weyrother system that I learned from a rider at the Spanish Riding School."*

He took a step back and said, *"Do not use that method on my horses, please. I've been to the Spanish Riding School, and I've seen horses that wouldn't even approach the corner because they're so afraid that one is going to use one of those corner exercises to make the horse do some-*

thing. I've seen horses that wouldn't even go to the corner, and I don't want that. I don't like that kind of training. Please change your method."

I was taken aback because the method was my go-to method for a horse that doesn't understand. It's very clear and it had been working great on all of the six horses that I was riding so I was a little bit nervous. I didn't know what to do. So, I simply disguised my method. I kept riding the same way. After a month, we were at another party and he had his glass of schnapps, and he said to me, *"You know, you're still riding that same method."*

I said, *"Yes, I am, because it seemed to be working so well. The horses were happy with me and I wasn't interfering with what you do."*

He said, *"Stop, stop. I've watched you; I've really watched you riding and I've watched the horses, and I ride them afterward. And you know what? I've learned something. It wasn't so much the method that I saw at the Spanish Riding School; it was the person implementing the method. When you ride, you're a very quiet and kind rider, and that method works fine with you. I've changed my mind; I like the method. Continue riding that method."*

Reiner had the kind of flexibility and open-mindedness that it takes to be a true trainer of horses. How many horses did he train? How many times was he World Champion in dressage? It was because of this flexibility. He rode the German system, but when he watched that other system, he said, *"Wait a minute, that's a good system too."* You know what, they're all good systems. They're all good methods, but the trick is to speak German to a German, speak Italian to an Italian, speak American to an American. They'll understand you, and right away most of your problems go away because you're speaking the same language as the person to whom you are talking. That's the same with a horse. Most of the problems are not because the rider is not good; it's because he's using a method that doesn't work on that particular horse. So I think it's well worth investing in education.

I invested a lot in my education. I didn't invest any money. I invested me, my energy, and my time in reading all those books. When I didn't understand a method, I found an example of someone in my area who rode that method and I went to watch it. When I couldn't understand the German method, I went to Germany and learned a lot about how much I had misunderstood the German method. These are the efforts that one has to make to be a horse trainer because there are no two horses that are exactly alike. When you run into difficulty, the fastest thing you should do is back up and try another method. Don't get stronger; try another method. If it takes strength, it isn't the right method. Back up, and go to another method.

If you haven't learned any other method, that's a shame. You should learn another method. Your own personal method that you pulled out of the sky and invented when you were riding all by yourself is fine, but it won't work on every horse. They developed many better methods than we will ever develop. Better to go back, study the classics, and invest yourself. You don't have to invest any money; it doesn't cost anything. Invest yourself. Learn the right method and speak German to a German guy and speak English to an English guy.

CHAPTER TEN
FLORIDA WINTER CIRCUIT

Every year in January, I would take six horses to compete in Florida. I usually stayed until the end of February or early March. Richard did not like horse shows so I was on my own most years, as we couldn't send a groom. He ran the stable and that allowed me to follow my competitive career. I drove the 36 hours myself, in the tractor-trailer, with whichever dog I had at the time. It was a long trip and I was tired on arrival. The horses usually were fine after a day or two, and I slept very well for a week. Whenever Richard agreed to make the trip with me, I was very happy.

There were some adventures on the long trip when I was alone. My dog asked to go out on the way home from Florida. I was able to pull into a rest area on the Florida Turnpike. I lowered the ramp to get a lead shank for the dog, got my dog out of the cab, and led him to the grass. There were always lots of elderly people in these rest areas, and that day was typical. A group got up from their picnic and strolled over to look inside the trailer at the horses.

One of the ladies then approached me with a question: *"Why did you let that gray horse out?"* she asked.

I was shocked by the question and I asked, *"What gray horse? What do you mean?"* Then I turned and saw a gray horse cantering up the middle strip toward distant Massachusetts. He had been traveling in the center aisle and had untied his rope by himself! *"OH MY WORD!"* I cried, running to the trailer. I flung the ramp up, threw my dog into the truck, and drove out of the rest area after the horse, heading north. But the turnpike traffic was at a halt because of the horse! I had no choice but to drive onto the center grass island and try to catch up. After five minutes, I came to the horse surrounded by a group of truck drivers, all afraid to approach him. I stopped the truck, ran to clip the lead onto his head, threw him on the trailer, and left into an empty Florida Turnpike.

I regret to this day to have not said thank you to anyone, but I was sure the police were on their way. As I flew north with my CB radio on, I could hear the reaction: *"Did you see that? Where did she come from? Never in my life!"* Later, at the truck inspection center at the border, I was questioned about an incident having been reported. I denied any knowledge of such behavior. I have never told the identity of this horse. It shall remain so.

After the first year or two, Richard didn't like to stay at shows so I was quick to learn to manage six horses alone. Luckily, owning a riding school, I had six sets of tack and I tacked up all the horses in the morning, hooked the horses to the wall, and showed all day. At the end of the day, I untacked, gave baths, unbraided hunters, and fed. Chores were done late at night.

Usually, I had no trainer but I was surrounded by friends who gave me advice. One year, at the beginning of the circuit, I was approached by Frances Rowe, the trainer of my hero, Joe Fargis, and of Conrad Holmfeld. She announced that she was going to be my trainer that winter. I was unprepared for that! I explained that although I would love her advice, I had no money to pay for a trainer. I declined her offer. She insisted, saying that I tried very hard and that she would train me for nothing. She did, and I learned a lot!

Frances always called me "honey," as she did all her students, no matter the content of her opinion. My best horse, Barnabus, was a Preliminary jumper when she trained me, and he was usually knocking down three jumps in every class at that level. *"Honey,"* she said, *"you are in the wrong division. Put him into the open speed classes starting tomorrow."* She could see that the problem was not the horse. I was riding backward to try to be clear, and I was bothering the horse. Within two weeks, he was winning.

Barnabus was a result of the PMU program in Canada. I had raised him from a foal. He was not for sale. After Frances changed my approach to his development, I refused some extremely important clients who wished to buy him, including the sponsors of the U.S. jumping team, which at the time owned the horses ridden by the selected riders. Later, this wonderful horse showed in the Midwest Grand Prix and also in dressage, initially in

Intermediare. He finally mastered the piaffe, always had a great passage, but was too hot to do all 15 tempi changes without a break. He could do three, then three again, then three again, but not consecutively. I still rode him in the Grand Prix, knowing that he was not competitive.

Another horse that I had at the time was also famous and a crowd-pleaser for all the wrong reasons. Fly American was an American Saddlebred with a characteristic high head and flat back. He had a remarkable resemblance to a camel due to his haughty expression and half-closed eyes. He was extremely ugly. He was also allergic to hay. He was desperate to eat anything green as a result of being deprived because of his allergies. Although he detested jumping the water, he was a winner in the Intermediate jumpers at 1.50m and usually paid the way for the whole group of horses.

With a trainer like Frances Rowe, I was eager to represent her well. In the schooling area at one show, there was only one vertical and a line of riders to share it. We all jumped one way and then returned in the other direction, with our respective trainers commenting as needed. The jump went up each time. One direction was uphill, the other downhill. Fly American had noticed a low branch of a tree, covered in leaves, that we passed each time. On the downhill way, it was within his reach because of his high head carriage.

As I turned to gallop down to the vertical, I saw that it was very tall, well over 1.50m. Frances waited with all the trainers at the bottom. As I galloped toward the jump, praying to find just the right distance, my horse grabbed the branch! It broke off in his mouth and he continued to the jump carrying it, with the leaves hanging out of his mouth. I was alarmed but I could not let Frances down. We cleared the jump to the accompanying cheers and laughter of the whole group of trainers. Frances was doubled over in laughter. She told me I had a lot of spunk.

When there was a water jump on the course, the crowd would always come to watch. It was never sure if Fly American would jump it or not. The crowd would always yell and make a lot of noise to help me. At one show, with lots of crowd noise and also a big drive on my part with stick and spurs, we raced to the water and... he jumped! But as he left the ground, he lost all forward momentum and landed at a complete standstill in the blue water. Because I had anticipated a very wide water effort, I had already moved in such a way as to be over the horse. When he landed at a halt, I was on his head. As the laughter in the crowd died down, Peter Doubleday, America's favorite speaker, announced, *"Fly American has gone down in flames."* Peter's humorous and imaginative announcing has added a lot to our sport over many years.

Fly American had a long career as a winner. Later, he competed in dressage in Intermediare and finally was a very useful school horse. He never agreed to jump the water. I never agreed to stop trying. He could also never learn the passage, which was a shame because that kept him from doing the Grand Prix in dressage.

Red Alert, an American Quarter Horse, was another significant horse for me. He was fast, stubborn, smart, and careful. This horse had been one of my junior's horses that we had donated to Kent School as he had become a little hard for my junior. As she loved the horse, we had agreed that I would buy him back from Pavel Blaho's donation program at that school, and keep him for his life. That gave my student the courage to move on to a horse better suited for her divisions. This scheme worked perfectly many times. Children hate to move on to new horses when they still love the first one. My school was filled with buybacks from Kent School.

Kent School Riding Program was one of the few profitable programs in the country, due to Pavel's inventive donation program. Donations of horses to a school qualify as a charitable contribution under U.S. tax laws. Horses were donated to the program often at the end of their careers. They would live a wonderful life as training horses at the school or could be purchased from there for a reduced price. Many of my students agreed to move on to a better horse if their first horse could be donated to Kent, bought back by Friars Gate, and used in our own training program until the time for complete retirement. Some of these horses never actually left home.

Red Alert was definitely of medium quality, but he was fast and won a lot of money for me. Actually, speed was absolutely the key to his success because he had a very short stride. One had to fly at the combinations and find the right distance in order to jump out. Once he mastered the method, he was a huge success as a speed horse. For a time, while Barnabus was recuperating from a tendon injury and Troubadour had not yet appeared, Red Alert was my second horse. He had no middle trot but could do passage. He was never competitive in dressage but mastered many of the high level movements. He was a winner!

Over the years of competing so many horses on my own, I was helped by other professionals. Lessons and lots of advice from Jack Le Goff, Katie Prudent, George Morris, Ronnie Mutch, and Frances Rowe gave me a huge advantage. None of them would ever accept remuneration! This exemplifies our sport and the spirit of the horse world which is always carried on by those who have profited from help themselves.

RIDING LESSON

One of the most important challenges to a rider is to improve the strength and performance of the hind leg of his horse. The hind leg supplies the power that drives the body forward or up, creating lightness in the forehand.

There are three main requirements of the hind leg: the horse must be able to put weight on the leg, he must be able to displace the leg to the left and right in big steps, and he must be able to push himself forward or up with the leg. If the rider works on these three tasks, he can completely control and greatly improve his performance. He can also make an accurate diagnosis of weaknesses, lamenesses, or obedience problems.

To put weight on the hind leg, the rider must make a small half-halt with both hands at the moment the hind leg is well placed on the ground and engaged. Rising on the right diagonal at the trot, the left hind is properly positioned to accept weight as the rider sits down.

The first test is this: in three strides, or three half-halts, the horse should make a transition from the trot to the halt, with the left hind ending up well in front of the right. Of course, the test should be done on the other leg as well. With an accurate ride, one can easily see that the horse prefers one hind to the other to carry weight. This is normal but must be trained until there is little difference.

To displace the hind leg, the rider must use his active leg when the corresponding leg is in the air. It is impossible to displace a leg which is planted on the ground. Rising on the right diagonal at the trot, the right hind leg is in the air when the rider sits down and is then in a perfect position to be pushed to the left by the rider's right leg.

IMPROVING THE HIND LEG OF THE HORSE

The second test is this: in three strides, or three leg aids, the horse should be able to move three meters to the left of his original track. Of course, the test must be done on the other leg as well. With an accurate ride, one can easily see a big difference in the horse's ability to displace his hind leg. This is normal, but not symmetrical. Asymmetrical horses are eventually lame horses. This must be trained in each direction until there is little difference in order to prevent eventual lameness.

To ask the horse to thrust himself forward, the rider must use both legs when the driving hind leg is on the ground. It is impossible for the horse to accelerate or push against thin air. On the right diagonal at the trot, the left hind leg is on the ground as the rider sits down, and is then in a perfect place to accelerate or to jump.

Finally, the third test is this: in three strides, or three leg aids, the horse should make a transition from a slow trot to a very forward trot. Of course, the test must be done on the other hind leg as well. With an accurate ride, while staying light in the saddle, one can see a difference in strength in the hind leg, or a tendency to lower the back at the moment of acceleration. This must be trained with each leg until there is little difference and ridden well until the back of the horse comes up during the thrusting strides.

These three simple tests will enable a rider to determine a weakness, lameness, or lack of obedience. It is sometimes difficult to distinguish which of the three is causing the poor response. Weakness is the probable cause of difficulty, lameness is the second possibility, and disobedience, the usual diagnosis, is rarely the problem. The performance of the horse will be compromised by any of these difficulties.

The work in the first two categories greatly improves the work in the latter task of pushing forward. They are listed in the order given here for that reason. One can seriously misjudge a horse's ability to push if he has not been properly schooled in the first two exercises.

The training of a horse is simple, it is clear, but it is not easy. The unknown and most important factor is the ability, precision, and character of the rider. Dissecting the areas to be developed in a performance horse makes the process clearer to the rider. It remains a painstaking task and will always be dependent on the work of the rider.

CHAPTER ELEVEN
WAYS TO TRAIN A RIDER

Most of my horses were normal quality horses, with their dressage training adding greatly to their success. Almost all of my jumpers were trained to Prix St Georges in dressage, and because they were sound, they lasted a good while. This made it possible to ride in the higher levels of show jumping with the medium-quality horses that we could afford. I again learned the value of dressage to a jumping horse. When necessary, I loaned a lot of my jumpers to other professionals to fill the Medal or Maclay classes in the U.S. Finals in Equitation, as they could be ridden by almost anyone. I also used all of them in my riding school to give my students an opportunity to ride the higher level movements of dressage.

I trained my riders to learn by watching. We had a game. I would perform a dressage movement on one of my horses as they sat and watched. I repeated the movement, explaining as I rode. After a number of repetitions, I would get off and call one rider out to get on and duplicate my ride. The watchers became very focused!

One day, the movement was the pirouette and the horse was my best, Barnabus. The students watched closely, I gave my best explanation, and Barnabus demonstrated beautifully. I dismounted and pointed at Gardner Powell, who was about 12 at the time. She leaped up, mounted the big horse, and proceeded to imitate my pirouette exactly! I knew she was trained to learn by watching if she was ever without a teacher. Students should not be dependent on their trainer. One can learn by watching and one can learn by reading, if one invests in the concentration required. However, learning with these methods must be taught.

Karl had taught me that a rider can learn to ride in four ways. He can take lessons. He can read. He can watch. He can ride a horse "while the saddle is still warm from the master." Because I could only afford the last three methods, I had learned a lot through books and through the generosity of other, better riders. Karl Mikolka and Reiner Klimke gave me a huge advantage by allowing me to ride their horses and watch them ride. Now, it was my turn to train my juniors in these methods.

Learning to ride by taking lessons is expensive and can lead to young riders who are dependent on their teacher. I always tell my riders, "You can depend on me to be on time, to answer any question, to get on your horse, and to advise you as well as I can. But do not be dependent on me. Only you can ride into the ring."

Reading takes initiative. There is no "one good book." One has to sift through all the masters and whatever is available in order to begin to understand. A rider dedicated to his sport will read. There should be required reading in a riding school to initiate the young.

Watching is a very good way to learn, but one must be taught to watch. My method of demonstrating and then requiring an imitation works well. One cannot watch and talk. One cannot watch and be on the phone. The ability to watch and learn comes from concentration.

Being invited to ride the master's horse is the greatest gift bestowed by the teacher. It cannot be bestowed by a teacher who cannot ride. It will not be bestowed by a teacher who is not generous. I was lucky to find two masters in my life who showed me how to train riders by their example. This impressed me so much that I have spent my life trying to teach as well as they did.

Karl Mikolka was taught at the SRS in the way it had always been done. The older riders instructed the younger ones. There was a rotation in the teachers and pupils. Karl told me that some of his teachers were tireless in their advice and explanations. He learned the most from these teachers because he was not a natural rider. Everything that he accomplished was because of a huge education, which he was willing to give away to any sincere young rider. He said that some of his teachers refused to answer questions and withheld the better horses in an effort to make progress difficult. He learned firsthand the difference this can make to a student. He told me, *"You will teach as you have been taught."*

In this way, it is easy to know why there are negative and critical teachers. It is the way they were taught. And it is practically impossible to overcome this as a teacher. I had been fortunate from the very beginning, with my Irish trainer Mr. Roberts, to my later trainers and friends who helped me so generously. This is to be repaid.

Regenerating our sport and the ethics of riding is a responsibility of all who have enjoyed the equestrian life. Not all give back what they have been given, but the list of top riders who do is long. Maurice Roberts, Frances Rowe, Karl Mikolka, Reiner Klimke, Katie Prudent, Ronnie Mutch, and Jack Le Goff are those who gave to me. My life was made possible because of their generosity. But there are many more on the list of sportsmen and women who are giving back. Denny Emerson with his clear and concise writings; Joe Fargis with his example of riding the horses for his amateurs and teaching all who want to learn; and Pavel Blaho, the immigrant from the Czech Republic, who ran the Kent School Riding Program, developing the young riders there to form the basis of many teams whilst riding donated horses. These people exist in all corners of our sport.

I decided to begin paying back to enthusiastic young riders with what I had been given by creating a working student program. This would create capable young professional horsemen and women. For the average family budget, the training of a junior or young rider is far too expensive. To be employed at a stable usually means long hours and little riding. It had become impossible to receive the training and the riding opportunities that it takes to reach the higher levels without being wealthy.

With my huge number of horses, many well-trained, and with my energy, I set out to find working students who appeared likely to stay in the sport. This led me to one of the most enjoyable parts of my life. Teaching had become one of my priorities.

At Friars Gate in Massachusetts, my working students were almost always American. Most of them are now in my world as colleagues. One of my first working students, Ian Silitch, had as much energy as me! After a long day of work on Saturdays, we always built the course for the Sunday Free Jump Day. Before I could leave, Ian would plead to get "just one horse" to try out the course. He was never out of gas. Already as a teenager, it was apparent that he would become a real horseman for life, and be able to do all the parts of the profession. Like Andy Wills with his palomino, he was never enthusiastic about dressage. He had his own spirit.

Others who became lifelong participants in the sport were Holly Brewster, Gardner Powell, Ann Thal, Ed Marcy, and, of course, Tuny Page (then Full), who discovered dressage after having been an eventer. I had lots of spillover students from the eventing world due to my long friendship with Jack Le Goff, the coach of the U.S. three-day eventing team. He sent students and horses from his world to spend a season with me to perfect their show jumping. Tuny was one of his big hopefuls, but she loved dressage and has since proved herself in that discipline. Later, when I moved to Virginia, Jack sent me French working students. He often came to Middleburg to visit and watch their training.

I learned from my students, just as I learn from my horses. One of my favorite students, Nancy Bliss, taught me inner strength as she succeeded in achieving her dreams despite battling health problems. George Williams' sister, Jennie, taught me about Nuno Oliveira, a Portuguese master trained in classical dressage, whom I never met. Her loyalty and warm remembrances of her teacher made me realize what a great teacher he was. Gardner Powell reinforced my conviction that imagination and humor are integral parts of teaching and training.

The atmosphere in a place of learning is what opens the door to progress. Surrounded by young riders on their way up, my own riding and the ambiance of my school went forward too. The house was full of students and we all ate together. We also did the stable work together, rode together, competed together, and took care of the courses and rings together. Everyone groomed, everyone cleaned tack. It was hard work, but my students emerged competent in every area of horsemanship.

♊

RIDING LESSON

Over the years, in the endeavor to master equestrian skills, we have passed through many phases. Depending on your age, you may remember some of them. Each phase had its merits, and none proved to be the panacea it seemed at the beginning. The phase of the draw rein, of the chambon or gogue, of the exaggerated crest release, of hours and hours of nothing but long and low, or of rollkur (which stands alone in that it has no merit at all). We have learned all these and taken some part of many in given instances, except the last.

Now, there is a new phase which needs to be discussed. The phase of the open knee. The popular success of this concept is based on incorrect or incomplete information. I will explain in two ways: first, the form, and second, what the result is for the rider's position.

A rider has two important muscles in the thigh: the muscle running down the front of the thigh, which should be close to the horse, and the muscle at the back of the thigh, which should never lie between the thigh bone and the saddle. This "back of the thigh" muscle is unstable, more so in a woman than a man, and will never support a steady position. The position of the thigh greatly affects the position of the seat in the saddle.

Normally, the rider's weight is distributed evenly on three bones: the pubic bone and the two pelvic bones. This is the neutral position, allowing freedom to the horse and agility to the rider. Once the knee is open, the thigh turns, the back muscle comes between the thigh bone and the saddle, and the rider finds himself firmly on the two pelvic bones only. Heavy, not agile, pushing down on the back, this position can never be neutral or easy for a horse to carry. But enough about form.

THE USE OF THE THIGH AND THE KNEE

When I was young, I remember well the comment of my good friend George Morris, who said, "Form comes from function." That really makes sense. A rider who learns function will always have a good seat. The function of the knee and thigh is largely untaught today.

In dressage, one is taught quite early to think of the leg in two parts. The heel, the calves, and the spurs control all the lateral work, flying changes, canter, and acceleration. The thigh and knee control the piaffe, passage, extended trot, and of course the middle trot. As one practices this, it is inevitable that one finds that the firmer the thigh and knee are, the lighter the seat is. As a result, the movement is enhanced.

For riding jumpers, there are two important functions of the thigh and knee. First, one can channel a wandering, green, or timid horse much better with the thigh and knee than with the calves and heel because the horse is not necessarily accelerated. If the distance is good and the speed is appropriate, but the horse is "floating," as they say in France, he is best reinforced with the thigh and knee. In my memory, the master of this was Alan Smith, and I discussed it with him a lot.

The second very important function of the thigh and knee is to control the weight placed on the saddle. There are innumerable possibilities for sitting on a horse. Rarely can one place 100% of the weight of the rider on the saddle of a moving horse without changing the quality of that movement. With an open knee, there are only two positions: off the saddle or 100% in it. With a well-placed thigh and knee, the weight is carefully controlled. Lighter is better to me; heavier is necessary sometimes. The modern seat is lighter than the older method because the sport and the horse have changed. One must be flexible. Accidents happen and a stumble or a rail down can destabilize a rider with an open knee. When the rider falls into the saddle, the horse loses a lot of confidence.

George Morris was absolutely right in his idea. The function is more important than the form. The form, however, should be understood. It reinforces the information given. I believe this phase of the open knee to be just that and, in light of more complete information and awareness of the function of that most important part of the leg, a better compromise can be reached than riding with an open knee.

1. Mr O'Malley was my best friend and champion. He taught me to sit *quietly*.

2. Richard Ulrich on Mrs. Gardner Fiske's Sporting Print.

3. Bunker Hill, a Quarter Horse purchased from my friends Ralph and Holly Caristo, went on to win the Speed Derby at the Newport Derby with Jamie Mann.

4. Cousin Rufus (above), a product of the PMU program, jumping at the Newport Derby with me.

5. Dorothy Morkis (above) on Monaco in the 1976 Montreal Olympics where she was fifth individually and Bronze by team.

6. Oliver (right) at the levade with trainer Karl Mikolka and a very novice me.

7. Cindy Mikolka (now Sydnor) on Lover in Brazil just before arriving at Friars Gate Farm.

8. Troubadour, owned by the Boris Terfloth family, in Quebec, Canada, in his early days.

9 & 10. Reiner Klimke schooling a young horse at his home in Münster, Germany (left) and competing in his home country (below). He said, *"It is not their job to understand our language, it is our job to understand theirs."*

11. Eliza Sydnor, daughter of Cindy Mikolka Sydnor, demonstrating correct stretching on Romm.

12. Thady Ryan, MFH Scarteen, wearing a collar on his broken neck with his beloved pack, the Black and Tans.

13. A depiction of the Scarteen country, seen from the hill above, with Thady Ryan on Jocko in the foreground.

14. Gardner Powell on her Colorado, a horse that won in every hunter division.

15. Karl Mikolka's student Joan Jones riding her mare Molly Brown in piaffe.

16 & 17. Karl Mikolka demonstrating the correct method of riding a young stallion (right) and showing how the thigh and knee control the piaffe on Aram (below). Karl trained at Friars Gate Farm for five years.

18 & 19. Karl Mikolka at the levade (above). This is an example of hind leg strength. I am on Topaz in shoulder-in at Friars Gate Farm (right).

20. The 10-year-old Mary Anne McInnis on her 11-hand pony, Mighty Mouse (left). She was a determined student from a very young age.

21. I am driving John Steill's pulling ponies at Friars Gate (below). It was not all work there...

22. I am riding Barnabus at a competition in Florida (left). Barnabus was a product of the PMU program and competed at the Grand Prix level as a jumper, and later in dressage.

23. I am riding Jan O'Donnell's Tarnished Silver in the First Year Green Hunter competition (above).

24. The gateway to a horse is his neck. Above, I am riding the Terfloth Family's Troubadour as a young jumper in a competition in Florida.

25. Ian Silitch demonstrating the joy received by both horse and rider after a good moment. Ian was an inspiring working student.

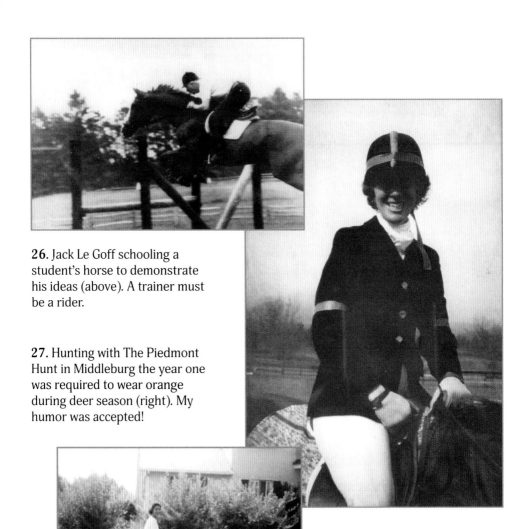

26. Jack Le Goff schooling a student's horse to demonstrate his ideas (above). A trainer must be a rider.

27. Hunting with The Piedmont Hunt in Middleburg the year one was required to wear orange during deer season (right). My humor was accepted!

28 & 29. Alev (Pepita) Sarc, a working student from Istanbul, in her "first day of work" photo, which was taken for her parents in Turkey (above), and Toni Subirana Flaquer, a working student from Barcelona, riding Bandit (right). Toni had an incredible eye!

30. Barnabus entered dressage
competitions at Intermediare and
Grand Prix just before retirement.

31. Dr. William McCormick (left), a lifelong student and practitioner of veterinary medicine, using both traditional and Eastern methods. Also a great friend.

32. Jack Le Goff, the coach and trainer of the US three-day eventing team, on the cover of the United States Eventing Association magazine (right). One of my best friends and advisors.
Photo © Fifi Coles and used by permission

33. My house in Bourgeauville (right), after the renovation, which took three years.

34. Pissaro, one of the last direct products of
Jalisco, was one of my favourite projects—
here in Florida for the winter.

35 & 36. My birthday present from Kevin Staut (above)—we were having fun—and the gold medal at Rio 2016 was a huge accomplishment for the French (left), and Kevin and Reveur played a big part in it.

37. The balance of the rider is critical to a jumping horse. Kevin Staut is on Beau de Laubry Z (below).

38 & 39. The quality of the gallop will produce the jump (top) seen with Kevin Staut is on Visconti du Telman. Bond Jamesbond de Hay is a lovely self-balanced horse (with Kevin, above).

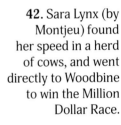

40 & 41. The château at Haras de Bourgeauville (above) is a jewel in the middle of Normandy horse country. Guy Jonqueres d'Oriola and Luca Moneta (right) make life fun for me, their collaborator.

42. Sara Lynx (by Montjeu) found her speed in a herd of cows, and went directly to Woodbine to win the Million Dollar Race.

43 & 44. Sandra Ball Markus (left), my best friend and technical advisor, emotional support expert, and fellow adventurer, and Kevin Messaoudi (below), who keeps my dog, Roberto, when I travel so as to give me peace of mind.

CHAPTER TWELVE
PROFESSIONAL SPIRIT

The group of professionals in our area of New England helped each other. We loaned our equipment and we shared our jumps so that each one of us put on shows with lots of jumps. We required all of our students to ride at the shows put on by our fellow professionals, and the ethics and protocol were respected by all. This paid off in an atmosphere with no politics, very little stress, and a solidarity between stables that I have never seen again.

Mason Phelps Jr. was one of the guiding lights in this endeavor of having a community spirit between show stables. His creation of the Newport Derby was a masterpiece of his imagination and courage. In an effort to help in any way that I could, I told Mason that he could ask me for any help. I was ready to contribute.

Right away, I could see that I would pay for this naïve offer. Mason was asked to appear on television. He knew that the cameras were going to intimidate him, so he asked me to go with him onto the set. We drove together to the studio, myself in the driver's seat, as he smoked something to calm his nerves. Upon arrival, I could see that Mason was very calm. We sat in front of the cameras, a question was asked of Mason, and... he froze, staring blankly into the lens. With rapid thinking, the cameraman swung the camera to me, and I blithely answered the question.

Back to Mason, for the next question, this time about the number of horses and their breeding. He was still frozen! The camera spun back to me, and as I was well-versed in the information, I gave a long answer, hoping Mason could recover. Later, our friends who were watching from home and from every stable in New England told of the great hilarity with which the program was received. Mason never unfroze. I answered all the questions. The cameraman always focused on Mason and then whipped the camera to me. On the way home, Mason asked me if I thought he had done all right. He could not remember a thing!

From this day onwards, whenever a publicity stunt was required, Mason and his publicity expert, Marty Bauman, would send me and Mason's right-hand man, Shep (Jerald Shepard), to do the performance. One of the best-received ones was in a tiny park on a hillside in downtown Providence. There were stone benches and three trees, but we managed to build three jumps in and around these obstacles. The park was across the street from a hotel and bar of questionable nature. We unloaded the horse and I rode into the park. It was lunchtime and people gathered around. I explained the upcoming derby. I explained that the very elite of the horse world would be there to jump, and then I demonstrated the course.

I had to duck under a tree and narrowly miss a bench but I had a clear round in my tiny park! My audience was fantastic. There were ladies of the night and good-timers holding their beers. Even the cook came out. They gave me a raucous cheer. Then, they insisted that I do it all again, even the speech to explain the derby. It was a sort of highlight of my career in public performances. The pictures in the paper were out in the evening edition, and I had to hope that the owner of the horse did not take that paper.

Every one of us rode whatever we could find in order to ride in the derby. It was the only one of its type in the USA. The course designer was Olympian Frank Chapot. The first time I walked the course, I walked with Buddy Brown, who had ridden all over the world, and we were really impressed by the height and the width of the jumps, as well as by the number and complexity of the natural obstacles. That first year, we all found that it took another level of conditioning. Those natural jumps were built on many private farms in order to get ready for the second year!

Mason was ahead of his time in so many of his unique ideas. Our group of professionals also developed the first, very prestigious, New England Medal Finals for equitation riders jumping lower jumps than those required at the National Medal Finals. This competition became huge over the years. It was a wonderful stepping stone to the higher levels.

We also developed separate divisions for maiden, novice, and limit riders, depending on the classes that they had previously won. The jumps were pretty small and my friend, Dr. Robert Rost, was disapproving when he came to judge one of my shows. He felt that we were diluting the quality of the competition by offering classes of lower jumps. From our local standpoint of view, this allowed more riders to compete, and all of our little shows were financially successful. Even the school horses could jump with the little kids. All the families were involved. A great atmosphere was created and many good riders came out of our area.

The atmosphere between professionals was our priority. We shared our horses, equipment, facilities, and areas of expertise. I rode horses for other professionals who rode less than I did. Mason loaned me an equitation horse for Mary Anne McInnis to ride in the New England Final when hers was lame, and she won the Zone One Medal Final for the third time and the New England Medal! I shipped all the qualified horses from our area down to New York in my big truck, saving the others from sending multiple trailers. It was a golden time in our industry and something none of us will ever forget. We bought oats and other staples in huge quantities to get a good price for us all. My good friend Ray LeBlanc went into the saddlery liquidation business and sold tack and riding clothes at ridiculous prices to everyone by coming to the shows with his van. It was not only the start of a huge business for Ray but the start for many kids in their first pair of chaps.

I learned that professional relationships can last 25 years or more if properly managed. Competition belongs at the show ground. It does not belong between like-minded people in the same business. Cooperation is contagious. The example set by us as professionals spread to the riders and their families, and created an unforgettable atmosphere.

CHAPTER THIRTEEN
THE SECOND NEW BEGINNING

The year it all changed began as a normal year. I took six horses and a working student to Florida, leaving Friars Gate with Richard, Karl, and Cindy. While I was in Florida, I received an invitation from Reiner Klimke to go to Münster, Germany. He did not promise that I could ride, but he did say that I could watch. I accepted the invitation and planned to go after the circuit in Florida was over. My horses could be on vacation. When I left, I had no idea how life would change.

When I came back, two months later, I was alone to run the whole of Friars Gate Farm. By myself! Karl had gone to the Steinkraus Farm; Richard had gone to the stable he loved, Dennis Riding School on Cape Cod; and Cindy had left to rebuild her own life. We had all worked to our absolute limit to create Friars Gate, sometimes at the sacrifice of individual dreams. Now, it seemed that we each had parts to add to our own dreams. Richard had arranged for a young couple, Ned and Brenda Doudican, to act as managers. They had been trained at Meredith Manor, and together we rapidly devised a system to manage this huge understaffed facility. I cut down on the number of horses as well as I could, but it was a lot of work for all.

I ran Friars Gate for five years by myself with working students. With the dissolution of all of our marriages, it became my goal to keep the spirit of learning and classical training unchanged at the farm that we all had developed. It was a huge test of my energy and a huge example of contribution to the stable by riders, owners, and parents. We competed a lot in New England, and I was lucky to have so many students to take an active part in the stable. Even with the help of a stream of a great group of working students, it was the hardest work I had ever done. At the end of those five years, I came to the conclusion that I should have a smaller business that I could handle in less than 15 hours a day.

In choosing a new location, I had three important requirements. I love history, so I wanted to be in a historic area. I love fox hunting, so I wanted a hunting area. I also needed to be near an international airport for my travels to Europe. I selected, as a possibility, the Philadelphia area, where I knew I could be close to my friend Vince Dugan, who was an excellent horseman. Long Island, where my best friends Holly and Ralph Caristo had a stable, was also a possibility, and, finally, Middleburg in Virginia, where I knew no one, was on my list.

First, I went to visit Middleburg. I never went further than that! It was exactly what I wanted. I put Friars Gate on the market. We had a huge sale of equipment and tack in the indoor hall, with parents of my students helping and making coffee and sandwiches for all. Furniture in storage, we left for the Florida circuit as usual that year, but with no specific home in Middleburg in sight. The old retired horses went to a friend to await my arrangements for them in my next life. All was settled; it was over. Driving down the driveway for the last time was a very sad time indeed. But my new life beckoned! It was a very good decision and one that I never regret. Middleburg became my new hometown.

As the Florida circuit came to an end, I had still not made arrangements for a temporary home for me and my horses in Middleburg. My friend and announcer, Peter Doubleday, with his usual humor, took matters into his own hands one day on the loudspeaker system at the show. He announced that I was looking for a home in Middleburg and that everyone should spread the word to help me find stalls. I was in the schooling area on a horse at the time. Within five minutes, I was approached by Diane and Joe Fiore, longtime Middleburg residents, to offer me their stable as a base until I found a farm! I accepted right away! Hospitality is a part of life in Middleburg.

Living at Diane and Joe's farm, in the apartment over the stable, I had the time to go and get my horses from Massachusetts. Barnabus was at the end of his jumping career, having injured his deep flexor tendon twice. The paddocks at the Five Points Farm, where we were living, were double-fenced. One could drive the tractor between the paddocks to mow. I turned my four retired horses out every night and brought them in during the hot days. I forgot that Barnabus would not stay in a paddock by himself, and I brought in the other three horses, leaving him to come in right after. Too late! He jumped both fences at once to change paddocks! Joe happened to see that and, as the entrepreneur that he is, ran into the barn to offer to buy him. I refused, of course, explaining that his tendon was connected by a thread. He was finished with jumping but still loved to do it.

Middleburg is a very well-preserved horse community only 90 minutes from Washington. The countryside is beautiful beyond belief. There are lots of dusty country roads and huge open-fenced fields, all paneled for the fox hunters to get across. Many of the old southern mansions are still privately owned. Middleburg is the home of the National Sporting Art Museum and *The Chronicle of The Horse*. Middleburg Training Track is well functioning for racehorses in training, and there are extensive polo fields, cross country training courses, and covered arenas to testify to an active horse culture. It's a paradise for people who love horses, hounds, and country living. And it is a friendly place where the eccentric are welcomed. Having immigrated from the staid New England atmosphere, where I stood out as too nonconformist, I was immediately at home in this environment.

I found a small farm by accident. I was told that a house and 10 acres were to be sold at auction in a very nice neighborhood called Unison. The owner had been sent to prison, and the bank was selling the house. I went to see, but the house was locked and one could not go in to see the rooms. There was a nice swimming pool filled with blackish water. I was so nervous as to what might be in the bottom of that pool that I went over to the Upperville Show, which was going on at the time, and brought friends back to look. I made Peter Doubleday dredge the pool to see if there was a body. Vince Dugan said, *"I could be very happy here."*

I went to the auction on the steps of the courthouse and bought the property. Carrying the keys, I went back to go look at where I would live. The house was rather Italian, with marble floors, and a dining room with mirrored walls. It was not at all what I had intended to buy, but the location was wonderful, and I found a barn builder and a fencing company to go to work.

I met my neighbors in a big group, as the Middleburg Bank held a second small auction at my house to sell the contents. I bought the enameled Swedish wood stoves, and I bid on behalf of the bank president, John Hammond, on the leather chair. He did not want to be seen bidding at the bank auction. I had to convince Aileen DuPont, my new neighbor, not to bid on the wood stoves that I needed to heat my home. She yielded and became a great friend.

My furniture arrived and I was home. The horses moved over from Diane and Joe's farm, and I made a ring for the jumps that I had brought from Massachusetts. My barn had eight stalls, and I had two paddocks. Life was a vacation!

The first year in Virginia, I learned a lot. I had imagined that I would escape the cold winter of Massachusetts, but I found that the Virginia winter was almost as cold, but shorter by far, than the winter near Boston. The summer was what was shocking and dangerous for my horses. Sun damage was a real threat to white noses. Horses out in the sun became bleached to the degree that they were not presentable. Flies in the paddocks kept the horses on the move during the day. Horses could only be out at night, I learned. The first year in Virginia, I learned that a horse had died of heat prostration at the Commonwealth Park Horse Show in July. I began to ask questions about summer care for horses in Virginia.

I learned about the violent summer electric storms in the early evening. These presented a real danger to horses, both due to lightning striking horses and the possibility of stampeding horses running into the fences at night. I tried to turn out after the storms. If a storm came up after the horses were out, and it was dark, I left them alone as it was too dangerous to try to catch running horses at night. I built run-in sheds.

I learned about electrolytes. I learned about the local hay auction, where the seller follows you home with the load you bought. I learned to go downtown to the stone wall in front of the Safeway store to pick up day help from the group of workers waiting there. I learned that my car was going to be covered with dust, no matter what I did. And I learned about snakes! They love a stone wall, and one must be very cautious. I was a community project, in terms of survival information that year.

The state flower of Virginia seemed to me to be poison ivy. It is everywhere, and I am very allergic. I had the worst case ever when the local boys that supplied my kindling gave me a load of dead branches of poison ivy to burn in my stoves. Even the smoke was toxic. The Master of one of the local hunts was Dr. James Gable, and he introduced me to the wonders of prednisone and saved my life!

My horses were happy with their new life of half paddock and half stall care. I saw the difference immediately in their personality and in their work. Freedom is so important to horses that they improve in all aspects of health when the ratio of confinement and liberty is in balance. This pertains to life in general and also to work under saddle. An underlying key to success is the degree of freedom available to the horse. I finally understood Klimke's ideas of lightness in riding.

In Middleburg, I made friends for life. Margaret Lee, a British lady who was the Head of the Foxcroft School Riding Department, was a unique character who upheld the protocol and tradition of behavior in the Hunt field. Once we were friends, she asked me to hunt the Foxcroft horses with the Middleburg Hunt as much as I could, in order that they would be fit for the alumni who visited to ride on the occasion. Gleefully, I accepted, and was met at the Hunt by Barney, her head groom, and a truck with my horse properly saddled and braided. After the hunt, I simply gave my horse in and drove home to ride the remainder of the day at the farm. It was heaven!

Margaret also invited me to use the school's cross-country course to school the horses that I was preparing for the eventing competition. My friend Jack Le Goff sent me young horses to school and hunt for a season, before their first year of competition. Hunting a season is the most natural way to introduce the cross-country phase of eventing to a young horse. Surrounded by 60 of his peers, there is rarely a horse who won't cross Goose Creek! Many top eventing stables are located in hunt country.

Margaret was a stickler for details. Her *"girls"* were always turned out perfectly, hairnets in place. She was an icon, and an era ended when she died in a carriage accident on my road in Unison. Her funeral was enormous, and I told the story of her broken collarbone in Ireland when I took her hunting there.

My neighbors were all involved with horses. Muffy and Doug Seaton competed in driving competitions with ponies at a very high level. During the competition, there are three phases, one of which is dressage. Muffy felt that I could improve the dressage performance of her nice pony by riding it. Making a pony supple which is between shafts is very difficult. I agreed to ride the pony, but I did so very early in the morning, as he reared a lot and did some other not-so-classical maneuvers at the beginning. I did not wish to be seen! Doug used to fly in the driveway to try to catch my performance early in the morning on his way to open the country store in Unison. Muffy has trained a long string of top driving ponies and is regularly an international competitor. I took her to Ireland to hunt with me, as she did that as well.

When I arrived, my next-door neighbor was Marilyn Grubbs, who ran a rental stable. City folk would arrive on the weekends and ride her horses on the dirt roads surrounding the area. One was advised to be careful when driving or riding when the renters were out, as they were often out of control. Marilyn sold me five acres and sold the remaining acres to my best ever neighbor, Carey Shefte, and her partner, Bob. Marilyn moved to Montana, where a realtor had convinced her that there was a magic valley with a microclimate where it was warm all year round. We carried on.

Carey Shefte was rapidly taken to be a Whip for the Middleburg Hunt. She is, to this day, a pillar of that hunt, both as a Whip, assisting with the young entry, and supplying horses to the staff. She also, with her partner, flies hot air balloons. This changed the life of our neighborhood. We all went up! We all waved from the ground, and some of us drove the chase vehicle in a pinch. There were adventures!

One day, the assistant pilot was to go up with a group of city folk. He was a very large man. He checked the weather, and all was well. They took off just as a squall came over the Blue Ridge Mountains, just to the west of Unison. When the squall hit the balloon, the balloon hit an electric wire and caused sparks and a panic in the basket. All passengers wanted to land immediately in the field below and the pilot was obliged to do so.

Chapter Thirteen

The field was not level and the wind was blowing, so he instructed, very severely, that *"all passengers would remain in the basket"* until the balloon was down. The passengers were in an emotional state.

The problem arrived when the corpulent pilot was himself thrown out of the basket upon landing! Free of his weight, the balloon flew rapidly up and away with the passengers! Screams from the basket could be heard from a distance. *"Pull the yellow cord!" yelled the pilot from below. "Pull slowly! YELLOW CORD!"* One of the passengers partially heard him and yanked on the cord, deflating the balloon. The balloon landed pretty promptly from the height of the wires above. All finished with bruises and a trip back to the city with a tale to tell.

The horses had to become accustomed to both the sight of the giant balloon and the sound of the gas used to control the flight. One did not jump in the direction of an ascending balloon. The horse could make a big mistake at the jump if he was staring at the balloon. When a rider was needed as ballast, that rider was excused from his or her lesson to go up in the balloon, as a neighborly gesture. The working students liked this rule.

♊

RIDING LESSON

The communication between rider and horse is surely a key to success in any discipline of competition. There are many aids which allow this conversation, with probably one of the most useful being the half-halt. The half-halt, originally credited to the French method, is greatly overcomplicated in the vast majority of manuals to the point that it is now rarely taught at all. In reality, it is easy to use and extremely clear to the horse.

A half-halt is simply a momentary tug on the rein, lasting no longer than one stride. It can be given with both hands simultaneously (as per the German school) or by the outside hand only (as per the French school). The more important information that makes the half-halt effective for various purposes is that it is directed at a hind leg which is firmly on the ground. This is much easier to calculate than it seems.

At the rising trot, having chosen the correct diagonal, the inside hind is on the ground each time the rider sits in the saddle. The inside hind leg is considered available to accept a half-halt at this moment. Similarly, at the canter, the inner hind is on the ground as the rider's seat goes forward. This is easy to find.

There are three challenges to giving an aid:

1. One must know the aid to be given—in this case, the half-halt.

2. One must know the moment in the movement to use the aid—that is, when the hind leg to be affected is on the ground.

3. One must choose the strength to use, which applies to the horse and the situation, when giving the aid.

A SHORT DISSERTATION ON THE HALF-HALT

The first two challenges are for the trainer to make clear. The third is for the rider, as this can change constantly. A half-halt given inappropriately in the direction of a hind leg which is not on the ground can cause a stumble or a spavin. The horse will rapidly learn to defend himself from this by stiffening his jaw and neck so as to block the rein effect. This stiffening is often misunderstood. It is easy to correct by careful riding for two weeks or so.

A half-halt can be used to make the horse put more weight on his hind leg than he normally does. A series of half-halts can change the balance of a horse from "on his shoulders" to "beautifully balanced" by putting more weight to the rear. There is no better way to improve freedom in the shoulder than to change the balance to the rear and then ask for a little acceleration.

A half-halt which places more weight on the hind leg causes the bending of the joints in the hind leg. The result of this lowering of the hocks and hips is more spring. Years ago, I was told to "put my horse on his hocks" in order to get more jump. It is the same concept, but more accurately taught to the horse and the rider.

A series of half-halts is a useful way to slow down the horse without killing the motor, as the rein only affects one of the hind legs, leaving the other free. A series of half-halts can alert the horse to an upcoming effort and, at the same time, prepare the hind leg that will function, such as in a flying change or in a transition from canter to walk. One half-halt can refresh the mouth which is becoming dull, refocus the horse that is losing attention, or quickly rebalance a horse that is too low.

The proof of a half-halt having been accepted by the hind leg is in what the horse is capable of doing in the next stride. Once a rider has discovered this, he will never underestimate the value of the half-halt.

Riders and trainers who have never really understood the half-halt do not teach it. Although this is understandable, it is a very serious and contagious lack in the modern schools. The overcomplicated explanations offered in the majority of manuals on the subject have led to discouragement instead of progress. In reality, the half-halt is simpler than one thinks, and with practice, can become of great use to the rider and his horse.

CHAPTER FOURTEEN
WORKING STUDENT PROGRAM

My working student program took form in Virginia. Not only did it solve my need for a workforce, but it also gave me the time to teach each student at least three hours a day. They made great progress. My income was in selling and training horses. I added stalls and then took over the next door barn. I finally settled on 20 horses as a workable number. We competed in Vermont, Virginia, and Florida, depending on the season. And we hunted in the fall.

There were rules and protocols designed to form professional behavior and initiative. No one was finished at the end of the day until everyone was finished. The slower worker was helped by the quicker. Team spirit. We rode in sets of four, three working students and myself. I taught and demonstrated. We all worked on the same thing but changed horses every day. Usually, sales horses were ridden by the students, while horses in training and my own horses were ridden by me. At appropriate times, we changed horses during the lesson.

As my land was in the Piedmont Hunt Country, and on a dirt road, the Hunt came by the door on the occasional Tuesday. Our rule was that we left the ring and joined the Hunt on whichever horse one happened to be riding when this occurred. Tuesday country, close to the kennels, was made up of easier and lower jumps than the country hunted on Friday and Saturday. Almost any horse could get across the country on Tuesday. Early on, one of those Tuesdays, Meg Gardner, later Master of the Middleburg Hunt, was out hunting accompanied by her friend, Jeff Blue. Jeff was new at the sport at the time and was hunting one of Meg's horses. We came to a coop separating two fields and Jeff had a problem. His horse hesitated, jumped over with his front legs, but stopped midway with his hind legs still on the other side. Jeff looked at me with huge eyes and cried out, *"Help! What should I do!?"*

I advised him to dismount onto the coop, jump back to the takeoff side, and drag the horse back to where he began. He did that. He remounted. *"Okay,"* I said, *"now we will jump it together, with more speed."*

"No, no," he said. *"I will go back to the truck. It's not for me today."* *He was pale.*

Jeff Blue himself later became the Master of the Middleburg Hunt. I took the opportunity to go back to that coop later in the day and paint it blue! It was not discovered until several weeks later by Master Erskine Bedford, who told me that he surmised immediately who had done it. Jeff did not see the humor in it.

Some of my French students really took to hunting. Cecile Grosse, now Madomet, was a very timid rider until she hunted a wonderful spotted horse we had been sent to hunt for its owner. She learned to gallop cross country and jump anything in her way on that wonderful horse. When she returned to France, she became a race rider and was named Third Best Female Jockey in Europe. Her children now continue racing for their stable and for other top European owners.

Charles Emmanuel de Rouget was made a lifelong honorary member of the Middleburg Hunt by his policy of passing a flask of aged Calvados to the Field at every hunt, and of hunting all the green horses belonging to Master Jeff Blue as a service.

When we hunted Friday or Saturday with Piedmont, a very good horse was necessary. I hunted Travel Along, my intermediate jumper, and was glad I had him. I have jumped iron bar gates many times, and after three hours of galloping in the turf, I was safe enough on that quality of horse. Jackie Kennedy, Liz Taylor, and Senator John Warner were often in the Field, along with top event riders and race riders. I was not alone in riding a very good jumper.

I taught my students survival tactics. When business was slow, I took them all to the Safeway store, ostensibly for groceries, but actually to find clients for lessons, training, or sales. It could take a slow round of the aisles, but there was always a conversation that led somewhere. As my students did not speak much English, everyone was eager to try out their French and we were also invited to parties and dinners on these excursions. They learned practical ways to meet people.

On one of those days, I looked up when a movement caught my eye. In the next aisle, I saw the head of one of my students, eventer Courtney Ramsey, a protégé of Jack Le Goff, flying by at great speed! Then it happened again in the other direction! I went around the corner to find Courtney, standing up in a grocery cart pushed by French rider Patrick Martin, who went on to win the French Championships after his stay in Virginia. Courtney's arms were out like a surfer, and they were going very fast. Other shoppers were cheering. We left with lots of invitations and orders for training!

Some of my working students were primarily interested in eventing. I tried to find opportunities in the area for them to gallop racehorses or ride steeplechase horses in training. Don Yvanovitch, a leading trainer in the area, gave this opening to Chris Newton, now one of the head veterinarians at Rood and Riddle Clinic in Lexington, Kentucky. Don called me after two of these sessions to say that Chris was a gifted race rider and that he should be thinking of another career. I almost lost a good student! The spring race meets around the Virginia and Maryland area are filled with top event riders as well as bonafide race riders.

My very first French working student was one of many sent by Jack Le Goff. Pierre Le Goupil, who is the designer of the cross-country course for the 2024 Paris Olympics, was a very tall young man from a family of horse breeders and riders in Normandy. He arrived on the day that Charlie Ziff flew his plane over his horse show at Commonwealth Park, throwing out hundreds of dollar bills as a publicity stunt! This worked really well for Pierre! He was the tallest person in the crowd, and his parents had sent him off with very little money. Laughing happily, he leaped up again and again, grabbing fistfuls of bills and yelling, *"I love America!"*

Alev (Pepita) Sarc was the Balkan Junior Champion before she came to be a working student at Friars Gate. Her great-grandfather had created the three huge Archaeological Museums in Istanbul. I showed her how to bathe her horse and take care of the feet after a lesson, and then told her to lead the horse to his stall. I laughed when she took the horse by the front of the noseband to lead him, and she explained, *"I have never led a horse. In Istanbul, a girl does not do anything in the stables!"*

A few days later, in a crisis of clients arriving with no warning, I asked Pepita to drive the riding lawnmower while I prepared the ring. I explained to mow in straight lines, started the tractor, and put her in place. She drove 10 feet and stopped. Turning to me with a huge smile, she asked, "Can you take my picture for my father? I have never worked before!" She was a returning student later and is a lifetime horsewoman.

Olivier Bossard, now owner with his wife, Nathalie, of Equi-Services Horse Transport, was a working student who came at the same time as Mathilde Menu (now Delaveau) and Laurent Delporte. Mathilde's father came to visit and unloaded a whole truckload of shavings. Laurent fell in love with a rider from Kent School, Jeannie Di Puch, and drove my pickup back and forth from Ocala to Wellington many evenings to see his amour. Olivier, after making history with the ladies wishing riding lessons in Middleburg, decided to return to France and find a place in the industry that would pay for his riding. He was the smartest of us all.

The winner of the Most Polite Working Student was Guillaume Blin Le Breton, a well-known professional in Normandy, who complimented my cooking. Toni Subirana, who now runs the big Centro Hípico of Barcelona, Spain, was famous for his ability to find the distance to the jump on any unrideable horse. Noel Vanososte, later winner of the South American Championships in show jumping, was a great cook, and we entertained a lot while he was there. I met everyone who spoke Spanish at every show.

Henri Prudent sent me Gregory and Fabien Rulquin and Virginie Genot as summer students—all teenagers at the time! I was horrified when Virginie broke her arm, but she took it as a sign of courage! The two boys were rapidly recognized as talented riders at a local show, and they have been so proven since. As well as having expanded Cheval Liberté into an important distributor of horse products, they produce horses, riders, and competitions of quality.

Henri and Katie Prudent were my neighbors. Henri loved to do business with young horses. Katie loved to win. So it came that Henri would drop off young horses at my farm to prepare to sell. They also dropped off horses at my farm for me to ride and show when they were away on tour. When Pancho, their head groom, came back with the truck to pick them up, I always made him promise to tell me how they behaved. Henri and Pancho both told me that they were so quiet that Katie put her ladies up to take lessons when the horses came back.

They also occasionally dropped off students who were unable to go on the tour. I met my future best friend, Sandra Markus, who owned one amateur jumper and one intermediate jumper, the latter for Henri to ride. I long-reined Sandra by the hour and rode her top horse until it was ready for her to take lessons in flatwork. We had a great time, lots of fun and hard work. Henri was happy with us, but he wanted his horse back!

We showed a lot, and the truck went out most days. When the show ended, the students rode home in the back of the truck, cleaning tack as I drove. Once home, the truck was cleaned and the horses were bathed by the kids, while I prepared dinner. Off to bed, and up early the next day to go back to the show, after looking after the horses staying at home. Once, I fell asleep at the red light in Warrenton, and the cars honking at me woke me up.

Teaching clarifies theory. By spending so much time instructing as well as riding, my theory involving the use of dressage to improve horses and riders of any discipline was becoming clearer. The program involving 25, sometimes 30, horses and three working students took all my time. I learned the importance of atmosphere, or ambiance, to produce progress. Energy and enthusiasm are keys to a good place to work and to learn. They must be generated by the head of the program. That was me and it was my responsibility.

RIDING LESSON

There has been a lot written on the importance of riding without stirrups and of sitting the trot. In order to achieve a perfectly balanced seat from which to use the aids, there is no disputing this idea. But these two sentences should really be the last two sentences in a chapter full of information on how to produce a horse comfortable with and capable of carrying a rider at the sitting trot.

Many times one hears a rider exclaim, *"This horse has a difficult trot to sit!"*

The response from the instructor can be varied:

1. Go slower.

2. You are not supple enough.

3. Drop your stirrups.

4. Don't give up.

All of these responses are slightly wrong. Here is why:

1. The movement of the horse should never be sacrificed for the comfort of the rider. That would be pretty bad horsemanship.

2. You are probably less of the problem than the horse. He has a rigid back and cannot absorb the rider. He has possibly never been properly taught.

3. Dropping your stirrups at this moment may make you even less secure, in which case you will grip and be even more uncomfortable for the horse.

4. Don't give up—okay, but change your approach.

RIDING WITHOUT STIRRUPS AND SITTING THE TROT

To start from the beginning, the priority in educating a rider should always favor the horse. Sitting the trot is a privilege accorded to a rider whose horse is ready to carry a rider in a full seat at the trot. The horse must be well warmed up at the energetic trot. Then, he must be made supple in the back, the easiest and most classical method being through the shoulder-in. It can also help prepare the horse, after these two steps, to canter and to carry the rider as he sits the canter, beginning with a sympathetic seat until the horse remains "in shape" when the rider sits.

The warm-up phase of the work cannot be skipped. From the walk at the beginning (read Denny Emerson on this point of walking the horse for a long while before working) to a certain time at the energetic trot after. Podhajsky, then head of the Spanish Riding School, told me once, when I had the great honor of sitting next to him during their Sunday Performance, that the young horses at the trot during their ride should blow his hat off as they passed. If you don't have the time to warm up the horse in your lesson, do not take the lesson.

Most of the time when the horse is too uncomfortable to sit at the trot, the problem is in the horse, not the rider. The horse's back must swing and be loose. The horse's back should also be round on top and lifting the rider. In shoulder-in, the horse discovers how to do this. The degree of the shoulder-in should correspond with the needs of the horse, not with the description in the dressage competition manual. All horses can soften their backs, raise their backs, and stretch for the rein by doing shoulder-in. The rider must have a feeling for adjusting the degree of the movement in accordance with the horse's understanding, as it unfolds. Before a rider is invited to sit the trot, he must be educated to this degree. And his instructor as well.

The sitting trot must be a real trot. If the trot is not correct, the work is badly done. There are six forms of the trot: working trot, middle trot, extended trot, collected trot, piaffe, and passage. In America, one often sees riders sitting on what is loosely termed the collected trot. Usually, this is not as energetic or full of impulsion as it should be, but is merely a slow and inactive trot. Allowing this trot is a part of the exploitation of horses that is becoming more and more prevalent in our method of bringing riders, who are not really educated, to the competition. Any time the movement of the horse is sacrificed for the comfort of the rider, real horsemanship takes a backward step.

The ideal trot for the equitation or young rider division is the working trot. Collected trot, properly done, is far too advanced for this discipline. Having warmed up, and having loosened up the horse, it remains to be decided if the horse is ready for a rider to sit. Here is an easy and classic way to decide:

1. Select the trot and the frame, or position of the horse, on which the rider will sit.

2. With no change of speed or shape of the horse, from the rising trot, sit for three steps and then rise again.

3. If that goes well from the rising trot, sit for five steps and then rise again.

4. If that still works, with no hollowing of the horse's back, raising of his head, or slowing down, try for seven steps.

5. Finally, sit for nine steps.

By sitting an uneven number of steps, the rider is again on the correct diagonal when he begins to rise. In principle, if the horse accepts nine steps, one can sit. If the horse is stiff, no one should sit his trot, as this leads to spinal issues and tension that will limit the horse's career. Don't give up. Instead, go back to the shoulder-in. Many horses, once in shoulder-in at the rising trot, can accept a rider sitting three, five, or seven steps in that posture. This is educational for the horse and for the rider.

I had the huge fortune of riding Reiner Klimke's Pascale, a many-time dressage World Champion, as a five-year-old. He was a little bit of a bully and would make his back hard as a rock if one tried to sit. Four years later, Reiner won the World Championship with this horse. I arrived on Monday after the win, and he told me to ride Pascale! I was amazed to find that he was the most comfortable horse I had ever ridden. Reiner never used draw reins. A horse cannot learn to swing his back, reach for the contact correctly, or find his own comfort in draw reins. Draw reins were invented for the rider.

The most important change to the rider who is learning to sit is that he must learn how to make the horse understand how to carry a rider. To simply force a horse to accept this uncomfortable chore, or to diminish the quality of the movement in order to make the rider comfortable, is not horsemanship. The horse must always be the priority. Once the rider has prepared the horse, one can say that in order to achieve a perfectly balanced seat from which to use the aids, it is impossible to ignore the need to ride without stirrups at the sitting trot. To skip the prerequisites and simply sit the trot with no stirrups is against the interest of the horse, and much can be written about this.

CHAPTER FIFTEEN
IT TAKES A VILLAGE

When I moved to Middleburg, I had no idea who I would call if I needed a vet, so I was surprised when a vet's car drove into the farm. The car went straight to my big truck, where a horse was living in a makeshift temporary stall. The vet got out, took a look at the horse, and walked over to the barn where I was standing.

"Hello," he said. *"I am Dr. John Mayo, your new veterinarian. I was sent by Dr. Richard Sheehan, who told me that there would surely be a horse living on a truck when I found the right farm!"* I felt a little less lost, knowing that my support team was still there. Dr. Mayo was one of the group of vets in the nearby clinic at the Middleburg Training Track. He was a serious and conservative vet, just as I liked. We became good friends.

When I arrived, I also met and liked Dr. William McCormick, who was a vet and also an amateur race rider. He insisted on riding all horses on which he was to perform a pre-purchase exam. I had found a horse to buy that I liked but was skeptical about his poor conformation. I wanted to buy him but was worried that Dr. Mayo would never pass on the horse, so I called Dr. McCormick! I borrowed a pair of men's work socks and pulled them over the front feet and ankles of the horse for the exam. I told Willie that I didn't want him to prejudge the horse. It was not easy to get this man to laugh, but I succeeded. I did not succeed in buying the horse.

Willie was intrigued by Chinese medicine and acupuncture. I had a school horse with bad hocks, and he asked me if he could use my school horse as an experiment. He wanted to inject the hocks with tiny hairlike pieces of gold. This method, he hoped, would make the horse comfortable for a long time and avoid constant joint infiltrations. Eager to be part of this research, I volunteered Bandit and was thrilled with the result. He stayed perfectly sound for six years!

Bandit came into play several times as Willie became a world expert in Chinese medicine for horses. Willie had heard that there are many nerve endings in the ear of the horse which affect the whole body. He asked if he could place a staple in Bandit's ear to see if this worked. I accepted but explained that I would be out of town for the weekend and he could proceed without me.

Monday morning, I asked the kids to get Bandit ready for me to ride for a few minutes before I used him in a lesson. He was pretty tricky to get on if he had not been ridden for a day or two. He was standing by the mounting block, ready to go when I came out. I gathered my reins, put my foot in the stirrup, and he turned his ears back toward me. *"Wow!"* I said. His ears were literally full of staples and, in the morning sun, he was shiny! I got on; he was perfectly quiet. He was unusually calm and easy to ride, so I got off and went in to call Willie. In retrospect, I think the horse was momentarily concerned with the weight of his ears. The effect wore off as the staples were removed.

Over the years, there were adventures concerning Willie. One night, the working students returned from a dinner at a Chinese restaurant with the life-size papier-mâché lion that was in front of the restaurant. They posed this lion in the hayloft door to surprise me in the morning. I had the reaction they hoped to produce. In an effort to avoid complications with the law, I convinced my next-door neighbor to transport the lion with me to the front lawn of Willie's clinic that evening after dinner. Willie's reaction was not like mine! He bought the lion a Chinese rug and placed him in the office of the clinic, on the rug, where he lived for years as a sign of Chinese medicine.

As important as a good veterinarian to me is a competent blacksmith. Good blacksmiths are skillful with a forge and ironwork, but especially skilled in reading x-rays and analyzing the movement of the horse to be shod, and clever in their handling of difficult horses. I try not to direct my blacksmiths, as they know the job. I do inform them of all that I see in my day-to-day work with every horse.

In Massachusetts, we were spoiled forever by having the well-known John Steill as our blacksmith. John was the official blacksmith for the U.S. three-day event team, which was based in Hamilton. He lived, however, on the south shore near Pembroke, and was a huge part of my success in keeping my horses sound and comfortable. He also played the bagpipes and drove heavy horses in weight-pulling competitions. He tried to teach me this latter skill, but I proved to be inept. As a blacksmith, he was magic.

When I moved to Virginia, I was uncertain about choosing a new blacksmith. My good new friends made a great recommendation in Chris Crawford, and he was immediately a member of my team. At the time, Jack Le Goff had sent me a group of horses to sell for the United States Equestrian Team (USET), as the new policy did not allow team ownership of horses. Each rider would supply their own horses. The team horses, Jack explained, would be sold. I was to remake every horse into another discipline, as none could be sold as eventers. This was Jack's effort not to compete with the private sector—an example of his ethics, which were part of everything he did.

Because I had a strong education in show jumping and also in dressage, Jack sent all the horses to me. The common denominator for these horses in their previous and new lifestyles was the basic dressage training involved in their work. So they passed from one excellent blacksmith to another, and from one discipline to another with lots of similarities in the basics. Jack had confidence in their new support team. Chris was not only a blacksmith, however. He was also the drummer in a small band! The band was coerced into playing at several of my parties. He also liked to hike the Appalachian Trail, and so did I. I have learned that blacksmiths are multifaceted creatures. It keeps them from becoming saturated with too much work. We hiked the trail many times as he prepared to do the Iron Man Competition, running all the level and downhill parts and walking the uphill. I was always the last to arrive in the camp for the night in tents. This spirit is an approach that I tried to teach my students as well. Life must be diverse to be productive.

It is always important that the veterinarian and the blacksmith for a group of horses get on well together and communicate freely. This has always been the case for me. I now understand that I was very lucky in my choices and that this type of teamwork is not always the case. Creating the atmosphere around the team is one of the huge responsibilities of the head of the farm. In the long term, the spirit of the whole group is what determines the progress. There must be hard work and long hours because of the nature of competition and the animal care involved. There must be fun, humor, and games in an equal proportion to make it supportable. There was this at Friars Gate and that explains the progress of the students and of the horses.

⚓

RIDING LESSON

The shoulder-in was invented in medieval times by the Frenchman François Robichon de La Guérinière. It remains one of the greatest tools available in the development of a jumping horse. Undervalued and greatly misunderstood, it is used far too rarely in the training programs of the modern competitor. Listed here are some of the huge benefits of this exercise.

Lowering the croup, something which adds greatly to a horse's carrying power and thrust, is a priority for most high level riders in all disciplines. During shoulder-in, the horse inevitably lowers his inside hip. I have always felt that my weight in my inside seat bone helps the horse to do this. My best coach and advisor, Karl Mikolka, explains that the horse himself will seat the rider to the inside as he lowers that side. This is clear. By working both shoulder-in left and shoulder-in right, the horse is painlessly and progressively able to lower one side and then the other. The rest follows more easily than you think! The alternative methods that one sees to force the horse onto its hocks with conflicting aids or stronger bits are really not necessary.

Less obvious is the possibility of improving the quality of the mouth on the outside of the shoulder-in. Because the horse is long and stretched on that side, the rider does not have the problem of the horse dropping behind, curling up, or over-bending, while the rider softens only the mouth. It is sometimes hard to isolate areas of the horse and he can evade training by softening in one area to protect another. He can soften his neck to avoid contact with the hand, for example. One can work with great finesse and non-conflicting aids to soften the mouth to the outside of the shoulder-in.

INVENTED IN MEDIEVAL TIMES: THE SHOULDER-IN

Shoulder-in is also the best way to liberate the shoulders. Especially horses that jump can change their technique in front by freeing up the movement of the shoulder. During shoulder-in, I tend to exaggerate a little the degree of the movement when my priority is the shoulder. The beneficial movement of the outside shoulder in opening the pectoral muscles is of obvious importance and almost immediate effect. It is amazing how much pleasure it gives to ride a horse whose shoulders function properly. It is not a surprise at all that a horse is more confident, more comfortable, and better on his feet when his shoulders are free. This could be the best thing that comes out of shoulder-in because of the effect on the confidence of the horse.

I had thought that was it until I went back to ride with Karl a few years ago. He suggested I ride in shoulder-in with a priority of controlling the outside hind leg and its track. At that point, you learn to keep the horse forward, which makes more possible all that was written before.

There is more, much more, because of the various sequences of shoulder-in: shoulder-in and circles, shoulder-in and renvers, shoulder-in and counter shoulder-in, and shoulder-in and half pass. These can vastly improve the agility, reactivity, and flexibility that one needs to compete in jumping disciplines. A whole book could be written on the shoulder-in.

"When you have tried it all, you will come back to
what was always there and look harder."
—Anonymous

CHAPTER SIXTEEN
THE LE GOFF INFLUENCE

I was privileged to have such a friend as Jack Le Goff, who was the trainer of the U.S. three-day event team. He had ridden in steeplechase racing and on the French three-day event team, as well as having coached the French three-day event team at the Olympics. In his very long career, he participated in 11 Olympic Games as a rider, coach, and judge. He could think like a horse and he could think like any of his riders. I was proud to be his friend and proud to take the group of horses that he sent me to be remade into other disciplines and sold for the USET.

Years earlier, Jack had invited Ralph Hill, one of his favorite riders, and me to go on a trip to France to select horses. On the way, he explained that we would be trying, among others, several Anglo-Arabs. I was completely ignorant of this breed and I assumed he was speaking of a horse descending from one thoroughbred parent and one Arabian. Laughingly, I told Jack that Ralph would be riding those and that I would ride the others. He rolled his eyes. Then, he explained the French Anglo-Arab. It is an ancient breed with carefully calculated crossings, not a pure Arab for centuries in the race.

Later, when trying horses, I found one that I considered really good, and I rode over to Jack to quietly confide my findings without alerting the seller to my absolute delight in his horse. *"Jack!"* I said. *"Buy this one. You can't believe how nice he is in every respect!"*

With a big knowing smile, he replied smugly, *"That, my dear, is an Anglo!"*

I was put in my place and we bought the horse.

On that trip, Ralph and I were allowed to buy horses as long as they didn't interfere with Jack's search. I bought a skinny bay with a good jump. When I got him home, he gained a lot of weight and calmed down. He became Savoir Faire, an amateur hunter winner for my student, Carol O'Donnell, Jan's mother, who also loved to ride. He was a huge success! Jan O'Donnell was one of my all-time favorite students who rode in every division as a winner! Jan and Carol shared a love of horses and dominated their divisions.

Jack took us to many of his old places where he learned to ride when we had found our horses. I had read a lot about the French dressage system as a kid, and I searched avidly for examples in the riders we saw. Not seeing any evidence of the method, I mentioned this to Jack. He told me that the pure French method was rarely seen due to the new shortcuts, and pressure to compete too early and sell as fast as possible. The classical method was being lost. I was lucky to know him as he never wavered in his devotion to his method.

When Paddy Be Good arrived at Friars Gate from the USET to be sold, he was just starting work after a tendon injury. I had no idea about how he had been ridden so I called Henri Prudent, my French neighbor, who had ridden him as a jumper before selling him to the team. *"I will be your coach!"* he explained enthusiastically. *"He will be the easiest Grand Prix horse that you have ever ridden!"*

Sure enough, he was. But there was a trick to riding him. One could literally walk to any size jump and there was never a doubt that he would jump it. But once you went at the speed required by the time allowed, it was not as easy to go clear or to manage his stride. Henri explained that I had to cut off all the ends of the ring and approach all combinations on an angle to make the time without losing the jump while remaining at this special speed. Always an enthusiastic coach, Henri would yell out, *"Turn!"* two strides before I arrived at the takeoff. I rode some big classes with the horse and loved him.

In fact, I spoiled him terribly. I left him at liberty to roam the property while the other horses worked. Customers driving in to ride became accustomed to seeing Paddy on the lawn or down by the swimming pool. Once, he loaded into the truck because the ramp was down! I got into trouble when General Jack Burton, a director of the USET, paid a surprise visit to see the team horses and came upon Paddy in the driveway. He came over to me to say that he was leaving but would be back in 10 minutes. I got the hint and stabled Paddy. Paddy found his forever home as an amateur jumper and lasted for years.

Jack sent me Kempis to sell after he had "tied up" due to stress at one too many competitions. In his final outing for the team, in Poland, he was required to jump up onto a small cottage on the cross country course. He always tied up in the winning position on Sunday. His team rider was David O'Connor, later President of our Federation and a top event rider at the time. He called me soon after the horse arrived at Friars Gate. *"You will never hold him,"* were his words of wisdom. However, riding in a ring over a track of show jumps does not present the same problems at all that one encounters on the cross-country course. I had no problem. I entered him in the Regular Working Hunters at the Washington International, which took place weeks after his arrival.

Kempis pleased the judges, Dan Lenehan and Rodney Jenkins. Kempis was a tall thoroughbred type, self-assured and calm, just Dan's type. He was third in his very first class as a hunter! I went home to feed at the farm, not far from Washington, and received a call from Jack. *"What is this news that I have received?"* he demanded. *"Is it true that you have entered Kempis in the hunter division at Washington!? He is NOT a hunter!"*

Jack was upset with me. He regarded the hunter division as an insult to his horse. I explained the nuances of the discipline as well as I could and how, in my opinion, it was a huge tribute to the past training of the horse that he could walk into a ring as impressive as Washington and perform over the biggest jumps in the division on a loose rein. Jack always yielded to logic. I went back to finish the show and Kempis was placed in every class.

There were two keys to Kempis' health problems. First, he needed to be in the field most of the time. Second, as Jack told me when he arrived, he could not be longed. He would tie up the minute that the longe was clipped to his bridle and he was led to the longe area. I did it once and never again. If one respected these details, he was a wonderful horse and he went on to be a fine junior jumper.

Kila 2 was another wonderful Anglo that I was privileged to recycle into the equitation division. He was fun to ride and a great athlete. Jack had trained so many horses in his logical approach that it was easy to find new careers for them.

Jack also sent me a lot of his event riders, for periods of time, to perfect their show jumping skills during the off-season. When he came to visit in Middleburg to watch the work, he would sometimes sit on the upstairs balcony to make the occasional comment. He was always amazed at the number of jumps the riders did in the course of the three jumping lessons each morning.

Because of Jack, I had my first French working student, Pierre Le Goupil. But he also sent me Courtney Ramsey, one of his favorite students, who came with three horses. Courtney was full of fun and energized my students into lots of social activity, while always showing up on time in the morning. I soon saw the similarities between the two.

In the evening, Jack would cook! He loved to make couscous and the kids loved dinners with Jack, which lasted well into the night. I never lasted until the end, and my riders were rarely any use at all in the morning. Jack was never tired. Courtney was just like Jack. We had a plan to run a school together for a while, in Leesburg, but the owners of the huge facility were never sure that it would be financially rewarding to them. Probably they were right, but it would have been great for us and for the riding community. In the end, we didn't do it.

Grant Schneidman gave me his wonderful eventer, Shoptalk, to sell as the horse no longer wished to risk his life on the cross-country phase. He was a natural in the show ring and won almost every class he entered. I bought other disenchanted horses from the eventing world for my amateur riders to ride in the horse shows. Lottery Ticket was my event student Dr. Maria Brazil's preliminary eventer, when he decided to avoid jumping into the water. He went on to be a big success as an amateur jumper for Karen Eisenhauer, a student of Barbara Miles. I had previously purchased the wonderful Jack Be Nimble from Tuny Page, as she moved to dressage, to sell to my student, Ellen Toon, a top amateur rider in both hunters and jumpers. Jack was a better jumper than he was an eventer.

I believe that a horse should be allowed to choose his discipline. The horses always make their preferences very clear, and a rider must acknowledge the fact that every horse is not happy in the hunter classes just because he was purchased as a three-year-old to be a derby specialist. I try very hard to see the tendency in each horse and remain flexible enough to go in the direction that suits the animal. It does not matter to me what lifestyle is the one that suits the horse, but it is important that he attains his potential in that direction. All the eventers from the USET found new and suitable homes. Some became dressage horses, some field hunters. It was fun to train them all.

The choice belongs to the horse. The education is the responsibility of the trainer. The privilege of having the association with a fine horse in a new area of life is only open to a rider who is flexible in his outlook. It is not horsemanship when the horse must be completely dominated to do the discipline of the rider's choice.

A good friend of mine, Ginger Klingenstein, sent me a gray mare to sell. The mare had a great jump and moved beautifully, but was a difficult mare to compete as a hunter as she had too much blood. One day, while I was riding this hot mare, the Hunt rode by our gate. As per our stable rule, we joined the Hunt and I was sure that I was about to die. Hounds took off, screaming, and we took off at the gallop, jumping a small coop into a field and flying up a hill to get a view. At the top, there was no time to pause. Below us, we could see the pack flying away from us in full tongue following a big red fellow, a fox we chased a lot for years. I prepared for trouble when we crested the hill and began to gallop the long descent to a large coop at the bottom. Imagine my surprise when my hot mare sat back on her hocks as she ran down the hill, added an intelligent step in front of that coop, and jumped in fantastic form!

We stayed out all morning and I let the mare pretty much on her own. She was about the best field hunter I had ever ridden. She was not hot, she was intrigued. I learned something. A horse will make it absolutely clear when the right job appears. This mare was about to become a wonderful eventer under the name Winter's Tale. She liked that job as well. She was not hot.

Kim Rehuba sent me a wonderful horse to sell when she discovered that she was pregnant. He was a beautiful mover and a beautiful horse. He jumped in hunter style. I learned by accident that the horse loved to jump the jumper jumps in my ring. I jumped up the bank and then the water jump, and the horse bloomed! I put the jumps up and jumped a triple combination with a horse smiling from ear to ear. Kim had felt the same and was selling regretfully. She told me that I was obliged to tell the buyer that every previous owner of this young horse had become pregnant upon purchasing him. At the time, I was riding a young jumper for Sally Smith named Cadence. She came often to see his progress and was thinking of having a jumper for herself, having won all three hunter championships indoors the year before. Sally is an avid horsewoman and loves to train. I had to have this one for Sally.

Sally's trainer and friend, Scott Williamson, came to take a look. I explained that the horse wanted to be a jumper, but I could see that Scott was not thinking along those lines as he watched me warm up. He wanted to ride. He put his hands up the neck and rode beautifully around my hunter course, smiling happily. I had to do something! I stopped him, and I insisted that he jump the water, the triple, and the bank, in that order, knowing that he would see the horse light up in enthusiasm.

"The bank!" he cried. "No, no... really?"

I insisted, Sally encouraged him, and he did it! His expression as he galloped to my bank is forever in my memory. They bought the horse. I saw it in the hunters at the next show. I did not win that one.

But the idea planted by Jack Le Goff, himself a passionate racing and event trainer, was invaluable to my future. A good horse can do most disciplines, and it is the horse that should choose. Once he showed me this, I followed his thread throughout my life.

RIDING LESSON

It is a sentiment shared by many riders of horses in the jumping disciplines that the quality of the canter will determine the quality of the jump. The canter is less easily improved than the trot. The ideal manner of assuring a good canter is to start with a horse that was born with a beautiful canter. Serge Cornut, one of the great experts in judging young horses in France, has given us the phrase *"un gallop utile."* Translated, this means *"a useful canter."* It is a very correct assessment of a canter in balance, usable by the rider, and pure at all speeds. It is easy to see that the French breeders have taken this phrase to heart. Initially, one educates the horse to do the movements at the trot, and then at the canter which will improve and perfect the horse at the jumping speed.

There is a list of dressage movements which have an effect on the canter. Similar to the use of antibiotics, not all movements are suitable for every horse's program. Penicillin, a miracle antibiotic, has no effect on Lyme disease, for example. As the trainer of a competitive dressage horse, one must teach all the movements demanded in the competition. When using dressage as a method of improving muscle, condition, and quality of gait in a jumping horse, it is important to use the exercise that corresponds to the horse. Another example of selective training is in the use of gymnastics for jumping young horses. There are many valuable gymnastics to do, but usually only one or two that are useful for any given horse. It is important to note that the wrong choice of exercise can be detrimental to the improvement of the horse. It is intelligent to give Tetracycline, not Penicillin, for Lyme disease.

Before attempting to use a dressage movement at the canter, it should

IMPROVING THE *"GALLOP UTILE"* THROUGH DRESSAGE

be taught to the horse at the trot. This stems from the fact that the horse is more balanced at the trot, and it is easier to give precise aids in the rhythm of one or the other of the diagonals. One of my best mentors, Frances Rowe, told me to never surprise a nice horse. Take the time to prepare what you will ask. This is good advice and has served me well. The exception on the list that follows is the pirouette, which should be taught at the walk.

There are many small details to each of the following movements which must be respected rigorously in order to achieve the right result. Done wrong, one can injure or spoil a very promising horse. Better to do less than to use force, and better to ride a well-educated horse under a good trainer than to experiment with your best upcoming horse.

The List of Movements:

1. *Transitions from walk to canter and canter to walk.* These transitions, where there can be no trot steps, teach the horse to push at the depart with his outside hind leg and then put all his weight on the inside hind leg to return to the walk. This is a prerequisite for a flying change.

2. *Lateral work at the canter.* This must be limited to leg yielding or half pass. Shoulder-in at the canter is not advisable for a jumper, and in my opinion not a benefit to many. This is not to be confused with shoulder-fore, which can help straightness. Leg-yielding is a prerequisite for a flying change and the easiest way to improve an impure canter. Half pass is extremely useful in softening one side of the jaw.

3. *The flying change.* This is absolutely imperative in a "gallop utile." There are many horses that can do this naturally, but a horse can be taught to do it with a fairly simple and calm method. An incompetent rider can make a real problem by trying to force this. Flying changes improve the thrusting power and the agility factor of the canter. Multiple changes on a straight line improve balance.

4. *The pirouette.* Fairly easy to teach, a pirouette improves balance, self-carriage, and the notion of being energetic without gaining ground. It is probably the most useful movement for most jumping horses, as the horse learns to come up through the withers.

5. *Counter-canter.* The movement most abused and poorly done, it serves very little for a jumping horse except to allow the rider to dominate the natural instinct of the horse. As I am against this idea in a jumping horse, I rarely include it in my program. When done properly, it serves to lower the inside hip of the horse and to soften the inside jaw. Dressage should educate a horse, not dominate a horse. The quality of the movement should always be better, not worse, because of the work chosen. If the quality of the gait suffers during counter-canter, it is not being ridden correctly and should be left out of this list. When ridden correctly, the huge benefit of the lowering of the inside hip is reason enough to leave it on the list.

6. *Jumping gymnastics.* It surprised me when Reiner Klimke told me that he could think of no better or less complicated way to improve the canter of a young horse than by jumping. He decided we should jump all his dressage horses! There are many wonderful gymnastics in books, but again, it takes a perceptive trainer to select the one or two that correspond with the horse at hand. Bert de Nemethy was convinced that the most important was the one-stride oxer-to-oxer combination with a very short distance. His priority was one short stride. By perfecting this stride, the horse was taught to use the ground as a springboard to improve his jump. The bounce, on the other hand, is a gymnastic to make a horse quicker, to correct over-jumping, and to lessen the use of the back in favor of improving the use of the shoulder. As it was greatly overused for the wrong horses over the years, we have become more discerning in the use of this gymnastic.

One of the many wonderful pearls of wisdom given to me by Jack Le Goff concerning the canter is that one should feel ready to jump an imaginary jump falling from the sky three strides from where you are. If your canter would not permit that, it is not a valid canter.

The study of the canter has always been of great importance to riders of jumping horses. With the increased difficulty proposed by our course designers and the emphasis on speed and agility in our sport, the difference between a good canter and an excellent canter now determines the success of our horses, as well as their longevity. The canter is the most difficult gait to improve. Its importance justifies the effort it takes to be informed and methodical in the training of a horse with a less-than-perfect motion.

CHAPTER SEVENTEEN
MIDDLEBURG LIFE

The level of riding around Middleburg was inspiring. Top hunter riders have always considered Middleburg as a sort of mecca. At the very local shows, one could compete with Tommy Serio, Olin Armstrong, Katie Prudent, Alan Smith, Rodney Jenkins, and Martha Sifton, all the best hunter riders in the East. Coming from the Boston area, this was intimidating. In New England, my hunters won a lot. In Virginia, I had to fight my way to be somewhere in the jog order. But I had the chance to learn a lot by watching.

Hunters are often longed a few minutes to allow extra energy to be spent before the class; this is the basic first principle of work on the longe. When I came to Virginia, I usually went to the show with a working student and five hunters. My horses were trained to longe four at a time. I could put my working student in the longeing area with four horses on the longe, while I showed the first one. Then I would take one from the student and replace him with the one that I had ridden. When all had competed, we waited for the jog order. I stopped doing this when I overheard a conversation between two of the top trainers. Within my hearing, not knowing who I was, they were describing my four horses longeing together. They were incredulous. They described me as someone from up north who did things in a most unusual way.

Later, I was approached by Kenny Wheeler, top owner and trainer in the hunter world at the time, to ask if it was true that my best hunter, Flair, actually lived in the field and only came in to be braided for the show. That was true, and Kenny went away shaking his head. I loved the hunters but rarely could get the quality of horses that were needed in Virginia to be competitive in the professional divisions. Because my horses were easy to ride, I sold them all to amateur riders where they gave great pleasure and won a lot.

My big love, the Jumper Divisions, were not, at the time, offered in every show. At first, I had to travel to find competitions. That changed and my life returned to what it had been in New England. I also missed the equitation classes for which I trained many juniors in the Boston area. In Virginia, there were many classes with so few competitors that there were no points available to the winners for year-end finals. My good friend Pam Baker, who trained many top pony riders in the area, used to borrow my jumpers to fill these classes with her pony kids. Most of my jumpers were pretty well trained, so they jumped happily around with a small rider over little jumps to qualify for the Maclay Final. Pam is a great trainer and her students rode very correctly.

There came a day when I recognized that the Equitation Division, which was so nurtured in the Northeast, was not yet in Virginia. I was judging at a two-ring competition in Western Massachusetts. The other judge was Gene Cunningham, one of the finest hunter experts in the world. Gene was a neighbor of mine in Virginia. My ring, with jumpers and some equitation classes, ended before his. I walked over to Gene's ring and introduced myself. I asked if I could sit with him as he judged the last of his classes for the day, and he accepted. I hoped to learn something. Imagine my surprise when we discovered that the last of his classes was a Hunter Seat Equitation Class.

The first rider came into the ring before the class began. We took our seats and the speaker announced that the class would begin with this young man, number 42. The rider picked up his reins and began his circle. Gene turned to me and said, *"Well, he's out."*

"Wait," I said. *"He hasn't jumped the first fence yet."*

"He doesn't have to," Gene replied. *"This is hunter equitation. A hunter rider never picks up the reins."*

My mouth was open, but nothing came out. I realized that I would have to reinvent myself to be Virginian. I have reinvented myself every time that I have relocated. The first time was when I moved from Minnesota to Massachusetts and changed my method to suit my new environment. The second was when I married and became a professional. I learned to put the work and the clients first, and my riding second on the list of priorities. Reinventing oneself is rejuvenating oneself. I have done it several times since and have never regretted the challenge it presents. Riding in Virginia was to cause an evolution in my career.

There were also top level three-day event riders and coaches in the area. Torrence Fleischmann, Wash and Juliet Bishop, and Karen and David O'Connor, all Olympic riders, were among many who settled in this area to be close to the many events nearby. The Middleburg Training Track and the hunt country provided the perfect situation for the training of eventers. There was also a big spring race season which drew crowds of enthusiasts from the surrounding country and from Washington. Tailgate picnics became a form of art. Many of the top event riders rode in the races as well as the spring events.

There was a special atmosphere in Middleburg in that the riders in all disciplines were in constant social connection. As a result, each rider profited from the others. The quality of polo, eventing, dressage, field hunting, show hunter, jumper, and race riding was pretty much consistently high. It was a stimulating life. I hunted beside lots of celebrities, all well-mounted on horses that could run and jump with the best in the country. At even the very local level, the horse shows were full of future national champions.

I did it all. I showed in dressage on my older horses that came with me from Massachusetts, up to the Grand Prix level. My horses did not compare in quality with those I met in the warm-up, but they were well trained. Barnabus, my retired top jumper, could do the Grand Prix pretty well with the exception of the one-tempi changes where he got too hot to do 15 in a row. I was intent upon riding at the level. My other two horses could do the Intermediare and Prix St Georges. Winning was not important to me in this area. Training was extremely important. Reiner Klimke had told me that any sound horse could do the Grand Prix. Some horses would be beautiful to watch, and therefore competitive. Others would do the test, but not beautifully. One should ride if it was possible. I did.

I rode in the Piedmont Hunt as my farm was in the Piedmont country. I also hunted with Middleburg Hounds on the Foxcroft School horses, with Orange County Hounds on whatever I was hired to ride, and occasionally with The Blue Ridge Hounds or Loudon Hunt.

In those days, I was running a lot as my method of cross-training. One day, arriving home after a local 10-kilometer foot race, I met an older couple in my yard who changed my life. Bun and Becky Sharp were the owners and joint Masters of the Nantucket Treweryn Beagle Pack, a foot pack. Bun shook my hand and explained their visit. *"Look,"* he began, *"here you are, an avid fox hunter and a runner, living almost next door to an old couple who can no longer keep up with their hounds. Please, be our Whip!"* I accepted with alacrity.

I love hounds. My dear friend, Thady Ryan, owner of the Scarteen, had taught me a lot about hounds during my visits to Ireland. Now, I was to have another mentor in Bun Sharp. I began to run two days a week with the beagles. I had a green coat and a whip, and was in heaven. I took beagles home, kept a few that Bun didn't want, and learned about breeding a bit. I ran at the Beagle Trials, and I met a lot of other enthusiasts.

Huntsmen Albert Poe (Middleburg Hunt) and Jim Atkins (Piedmont Hunt) with his wife, K.T., were invaluable sources of information and had colorful stories about the history and evolution of hunting in the area. One afternoon, on a ride over the mountain to get a hound, Albert told me of how the deer problem (hounds running after deer instead of the hunted fox) evolved. He explained that deer were almost extinct in Loudon County at one point. The county decided to plant deer on the mountain between Upperville and Paris, Virginia, to replenish the deer population as it once was. This plan worked well, but soon the occasional deer was seen by hounds when the Hunt was in Upperville. Never having been schooled against hunting deer, Albert, then the Huntsman for the Piedmont, began to lose hounds who hunted the deer back up the mountain.

After every hunt, Albert was obliged to put away those hounds he had controlled and drive the hound truck up the mountain, into moonshine territory, blowing his horn out the window, and asking anyone he saw if stray hounds had been seen. The locals became very cooperative in finding hounds when Albert began to pay $5 each for captured hounds. The day Albert finally realized that he must retrain his hounds was the day one of the mountain men offered him $10 for his horn. This was about to cost the Hunt a lot of money!

Occasionally, we had the same problem with the beagles. Beagles are enthusiastic and very optimistic. This nature explains why a small beagle frantically chases a big deer. Bun and I were standing together, listening to the pack hunting a grove in front of us, when suddenly the cry of the hounds changed to another pitch. He turned to me and said one word: *"DEER!"* The pack had turned and were racing directly away from us, out of the copse and up the hill, into the open on the other side from where we were listening. Bun looked at me and simply said, *"YOU BETTER GET RUNNING!"* Egad!

I was to outrun a disappearing pack of beagles running full speed after a deer. I flew. I flew for miles. I learned that I was not a fast runner, but could keep going for a long time. The pack was stopped by a savvy fox hunter in a pickup truck. It takes a village. I caught up and thanked him profusely. We went home in disgrace. Thank goodness the Beagle Institute, where the National Trials are held, is fenced to be deer-proof so as to avoid this unhappy situation at the competition.

Jim and K.T. were Huntsman and Whip at the Piedmont Hunt and lived close to me at the kennels. Jim was a very tall fellow and I always tried to find him horses to use as, in my opinion, the Hunt gave him horses which were too small. He and K.T. let me walk out with hounds and help with the young entry while coupled. They were happy with another hand, and I was thrilled to get to know the hounds. Jim was a great huntsman and a fine gentleman. It was a good time for the Piedmont Hunt.

I never did play polo. I don't consider it a horse sport. It is a ball game, and the horses are a means to play. The occasional pony is loved. More often, they are treated as a pack and are used rather indiscriminately to win the game.

I wanted to ride the spring races. I tried to learn the science of it by going to all the races one season with Ready Snodgrass, a good lady jockey. She explained a lot of the risks to try to avoid. It was easy to have a bad fall by being beside a horse who left the ground at a jump and, in doing so, encouraged your own horse to jump early. It is easy to get boxed in. I saw a lot that I had not seen from the grandstand.

Donny Yovanovitch, a good trainer of jump racers, kindly invited me to his field to try to ride a hurdle horse. He sent me down to the end of the field and instructed me to jump the three hurdles at top speed, finishing where he would be standing. His last and only words of advice were, *"Do not drop his head!"*

I cantered down to the end, the horse getting hot as I turned for the run home. We raced at the first hurdle at what I considered breakneck speed. Donny later referred to this speed as a *"morning canter on the paths."* My horse rose only slightly to jump the hurdle and hit it with front and hind legs resoundingly, galloping on to the next.

"Wow," I thought. *"He didn't really jump, I hope I didn't hurt him!"* The horse flew on, jumped the second with a loud clattering of rails, nothing broken, and then the last, hitting both front and hind. I galloped up to Donny and apologized profusely.

"No!" he said, laughingly. *"That was great! You don't lose time in the air."* The feeling of this type of jump was completely foreign to what I knew. I thanked Donny profusely for his generosity and went home to think. In the end, I decided not to race. It was not natural to me and therefore too dangerous. I was an avid spectator.

I did event once. When I called my friend Jack Le Goff after I had won the training level, he was unhappy. *"No more!"* he said. *"That's enough. Please don't ride in eventing!"* I respectfully resigned from that idea.

We competed in Vermont all summer, living in the condominiums used for the skiers all winter. Every day, after the show, I hiked up to the top of our mountain and back. My friends, John and Dottie Ammerman, were the show organizers and the atmosphere was wonderful.

In the fall, we competed in Virginia and hunted. In the winter, we showed in Florida to avoid the weather. All working students rode in every show that I did! To the French students, the 22-hour drive to the Florida show was completely crazy, but they loved the idea when they arrived. In the spring, we competed in Virginia again.

RIDING LESSON

Why are you longeing the horse? What is to be accomplished by that? As in every phase of training, the objective while longeing should be clear to the handler and to the horse so as to avoid endless repetitive circles or efforts. There are four main objectives while longeing and these must be clear and well-considered before the work begins.

First, one can longe a horse to give him the opportunity to play, move freely, and warm up with no weight on his back. This gives the trainer time in which he can observe the horse on a large circle while he is free. The longe line should be 10 meters, not eight, but the trainer can move if the longe line is a short one. No horse can move freely on a circle of less than twenty meters. The horse should have no side reins, and be allowed to pick his gait. He should move in both directions, starting with the direction of his preference.

When the horse bucks and plays, he must not run against a fixed rein, in order to avoid injury. The trainer must move with the horse and bring him back smoothly. One can easily see the natural balance of the horse, the gait of preference, the use of the horse's neck and back, the difference between the movement to the right from the movement to the left, and the apparent soundness of the horse. In a serious approach to any horse, this is five to 10 minutes well spent every day, by a competent trainer.

Second, one can longe a horse to purify his gaits. This is the only time in longeing the horse when repetition is necessary. It is useful with a horse who is not regular or stable in his cadence. The longe line should again be 10 meters long. It is better if the trainer stays on one point to ensure that the circle is absolutely round. The objective is to let the horse

THE MAGIC OF
THE LONGE LINE

find his rhythm in each gait himself. He has found that rhythm when the number of strides is the same on each succeeding circle. The side reins can be adjusted in several ways. They can establish a limit to the space accorded to the position of the neck. They can give support to a horse who needs a more secure feeling. They can establish a bend to the inside or to the outside, always between the shoulders, depending on which improves the purity of the gait.

The bend to the inside can stop the action of the inside shoulder or the inside hind leg, but can teach the horse to yield his neck. The bend to the outside can free the inside shoulder and inside hind leg, explaining the immediate improvement of a horse with an impure canter, or simply give a young horse a little support with the outside rein at the canter. The side reins must never produce a horse which is behind the vertical in his head carriage. A horse behind the vertical in his head carriage is a horse behind the rider. It is extremely important not to train a mistake that must be corrected later by a rider.

Third, one can longe a horse in order to educate him to an aid which will be used later by a rider. There are many examples of this more sophisticated use of the longe. It is an easy and good beginning to teach the horse to lower his neck and reach forward to the hand of the trainer on command. With a bend to the inside and a slight displacement of the haunches to the outside, every horse will lower his neck in a very short time. The rider can then use the same positioning to produce the same movement—a very important escape valve when a horse is becoming too short in the neck later.

A horse can be easily taught to yield in the atlas region of his neck by the trainer touching the inside mouth of the horse every time that the inside fore touches the ground. Many problems of connection with the mouth are actually caused by rigidity in the atlas region, usually resulting in tongue problems or a horse behind the vertical. A horse will rarely resist the inside hand of the rider if it is coordinated with the inside foreleg, because he is stabilized by its position on the ground.

In these two examples of training the horse on the longe, no side reins are useful. The longe should be attached to the inside ring of a plain snaffle. There are many more examples of training the horse to an aid which he finds confusing by teaching it on the longe. One has the advantage of watching one's effect.

Finally, fourth, one can longe a horse with a rider to educate the rider or to educate the horse. There are many possibilities. The horse can learn, once he can longe in balance, to carry a rider on the same circle. The horse must adjust his balance, and the rider must sit correctly with no influence. Also, a rider can be given one responsibility while the trainer takes another. In this way, the rider has less than his usual work and can concentrate on perfecting one aid at a time. If the rider is to use his legs to support the movement forward, the trainer can use his hand to contain the horse. If the rider is to use his outside rein to control the speed or to give support, the trainer can use his inside rein, the longe, to correct the bending. If the rider is responsible for the quality of the connection with the mouth of the horse, the trainer can take, with his longe whip, the responsibility of impulsion and forward thinking to avoid the horse becoming behind the vertical. A rider who has been trained on the longe is an asset to any team but a rare find today.

Another type of work on the longe is jumping training. On the longe, the horse is not encumbered by a rider but still controlled by the trainer. A useful intermediate step between free jumping and mounted jumping, this can facilitate the work for the future rider. The trainer can control the speed and the distance easily from the ground. He can see the style of the horse and determine which speed and which distance produces the nicest jump. Later, he can use this information to build the appropriate gymnastics for this same horse.

Longeing is a huge part of training a horse. It is greatly misused as a method of tiring out a fresh horse or confining the horse with artificial reins into a false silhouette. Because of its flagrant misuse, longeing has taken on a bad connotation. It is not for a beginner nor a groom, but for a focused trainer. It is a very important skill.

CHAPTER EIGHTEEN
THE THIRD NEW BEGINNING

It was a full life and a fun life. It could have lasted forever but for a conversation I had with my parents. I invited my parents to dinner at a restaurant that my mother loved. On the phone, I explained that I would do the driving, there would be no problem with getting a reservation, and it would be fun. My mom asked me which night I had chosen and I replied, *"Thursday! No noisy crowd, plenty of parking."*

"Oh, no..." she demurred. *"We can't go out on Thursdays."*

"Why not?" I asked in surprise.

"We have TV programs," was the excuse.

Seinfeld won the contest.

I thought about this and I thought about my life. I was at a crossroads. I could go on, up and down the coast, showing and hunting and repeating. Or... I could try something exciting and challenging.

What if, I imagined, I would move to a foreign land where few people knew me, and where I did not speak the language? The question I posed to myself was: how long would it take to arrive at the same level of success I enjoyed in America in my field under those conditions? I would put myself in a sort of self-imposed outward-bound program.

After a lot of thought, I chose France. The easiest horse in the world to ride is the French one, and I had ridden a lot of them. Germany was too cold for me. I had a few working students to help me in France in an emergency. And I love cheese!

I shocked all my neighbors, friends, and students when I announced my decision to move to France and start over. I knew I would be reinventing myself, but always with horses, so what could go wrong? The minute I had made and announced my decision, it felt like exactly the right thing to do. I sold my vehicles, put the furniture in storage, arranged with an agent to rent the farm, and packed my bags. I would land at Haras de Boele, in Normandy, where my student Patrick Martin was training. From that safety point, I would see where I would like to locate myself. I planned to teach and to train horses as I had done in America.

I took my dogs, Wayne and Caroline—both males, named after Wayne and Caroline Fennimore. Caroline was my amateur hunter rider, a working student of sorts, and Wayne was a strong supporter and advisor. The dogs would learn to speak French and carry baguettes. We all had three-month tourist visas. My best neighbors and friends, Carey Schefte and Sandra Markus, drove me and the dogs to the plane, shaking their heads and promising to visit.

Life in France began in the countryside around L'Aigle, in the lost department of L'Orne. Haras de Boele was a beautiful stud farm with a château, a small track, and loads of pastures. The barns were brick and divided into groups of four enormous boxes, each group with its own aisle. There were about 60 boxes and it was incredibly difficult to keep the yard clean. All were bedded on straw, and the stalls were bedded daily but completely emptied and re-bedded once a week.

I could teach Patrick and Carine Dussault, the daughter of the owners, and go to the shows with them to become acquainted with the system. Young horses competed only on Tuesday, Wednesday, and Thursday. Normal classes were often held at a different location on Friday, Saturday, and Sunday. One needed a license to ride, and also a license to teach.

I could get the license to ride easily, but it became immediately apparent that I could not have a license to teach unless I spent at least a year doing a formation. Even with an extensive dossier of recommendations from all my American friends, nothing was possible. It was all based on the National Health System. Any accident in France resulting in medical aid is paid for by the National Health System. Therefore, all instructors must be licensed and trained in first aid and safety procedures to the satisfaction of the government. The problem was not in my competence as a teacher but in my training in accident prevention and first aid. My first idea of teaching in France was blocked. I would concentrate on the training of young horses and coaching at shows.

Very quickly, I found a problem in these ideas as well. At that point, coaching was done for no remuneration as a service to one's clients. Also, the young horses were trained by the breeders by free jumping at home, and many times, shipped to the show to find a rider to catch a ride at the competition. The economy was such that no one could afford training. Advice was given freely. People solved their own problems. No one took lessons. I was in a different world! I needed to figure out a plan to make a living.

The first young horse show that I went to see was in Bayeux. I arrived early and found a grass field, recently mowed but not raked, fenced in wire, and empty. After a time, a tractor arrived, pulling a huge wagon full of jumps, and kids on top of the jumps. The wagon circled the field and the kids built the jumps at the direction of the driver. They were placed here and there. Later, the driver got down and put numbers on the jumps. Voilà! The early French course designer was born. My mouth was open. I had just come from Wellington, where the course designer had been Pamela Carruthers.

The young horses arrived in trailers pulled by tractors as well as by cars. Some horses were ridden to the show. Two or three were led over, saddled, to look for a willing jockey. One young stallion arrived being led by two strong men, one on each side, with shanks attached to his bridle. They found a rider and led the horse into the field to turn him loose. The two men blocked the gate and the catch rider tried to get the horse into a place where he could see jump number one. Being free-schooled, once these young horses see a jump, they go on their own. The horse finished the course, and the men caught him up and led him off the field. My mouth was still open.

Patrick and his wife Babette had bought a son of Quidam de Revel, Bhakti de Beaupre, that they wanted me to ride. The goal was to sell the young stallion to the National Stud at the end of the year. He was a beautiful mover and a good but not terribly careful jumper. I was thrilled to have the project. We went to Saint-Lô. I had seen pictures of the show, with the long ring in grass, divided by alleys made in sand. The jumps were all placed on the alleys. This made it remarkably easier to ride an uneducated horse around the course, which was big. Big was good for Bhakti, as he needed to be impressed. The ring was on a substantial slope. One began downhill in my class, then after six or seven jumps, a turn around, and the remaining jumps up the hill, always on the alleys. I chose a rather strong snaffle and was glad of it. As I entered the famous ring on such a nice horse in the Normandy sun, I smiled broadly.

At the day's end, there was a meeting called by the riders. They wanted to discuss, with the Haras National of Saint-Lô, the remaking of the ring and the elimination of those alleys. Had I been able to speak French, I would have spoken of the tradition and the worldwide fame of that ring, but I would have been overruled. Patrick explained to me that the horses became dependent on the alleys and were impossible to ride elsewhere. I had not thought of that. It was beautiful.

I remade one of the many unused apartments over the stable for me. It was a lovely apartment and I was ready to take a working student. Voilà, Camille Crawford, whose father was the Master of Fox Hounds at the Potomac Hunt in Maryland. Camille was my right-hand girl, rode a lot, bought a great jumper, and went back to civilization. She opened the doors for many others.

Meanwhile, I was training Carine Dussault on her excellent six-year-old mare, Altesse du Boele, by Narcos. Carine's parents, who owned the Haras, were very supportive of her daily training sessions and the preparation for Carine to ride her own mare in the Young Horse Finals in Fontainebleau. The jumps were huge on that day. There were not many amateurs riding in the six-year-old finals, but we had a brave mare and a determined team. Carine ended up 25th in the finals out of hundreds, and we decided to go to Wellington in the winter. The mare would be for sale. After Wellington, I felt that I would start on my own, but my French was not progressing as it should. Patrick, Babette, and Carine all spoke English. I needed to relocate! I had fallen in love with the area around Deauville so I hoped to find a place there. By coincidence, there was an opening.

Madame Dauzier called me to ask if I would come to Deauville to discuss the training of her daughter, Marie Charlotte, who wished to be a professional. A stable had been built beside one of the racetracks for Marie Charlotte, and a trainer was needed. I took the job and rented stalls at the race track for my own horses. It was fun and challenging because we needed to buy horses for Marie and sell them to satisfy the business aspect of professional life. Marie was to be the rider. We bought two three-year-olds at the Fences Sale, and some older horses, and began to train.

At the same time, I began to realize that teaching in my habitual manner would not be possible in France, nor would my training of young horses. I decided to become a horse dealer. Why not? I was in the middle of horse-breeding Normandy and horses must be for sale. I went to a show, found a five-year-old I liked, and, in my broken French, asked its owner, Germain Levallois, if it was for sale. He took a step back. He regarded me with an uncomfortable expression. Then he looked around us and asked if my husband was nearby! I explained that I was alone and that I was the buyer. He said the horse was not for sale.

This happened several times as I approached the older French breeders Fernand Leredde, Alain Navet, and Alexis Pignolet. I realized that as a woman horse dealer, I was out of place in Normandy. I would start to approach the riders instead of the owners as they were younger. It worked! All horses were suddenly for sale. I bought a few, educated them in the American system, and sold them to friends in the USA. Soon, I had a way to earn my way, reinvented as a horse dealer.

In this manner, I began to meet people and discover the places to find horses in France, and later in Europe. I started by going to shows in France. At a night show in Caen, I was to watch the big class of the day, a speed class of 1.40m. The jumps were easily 1.45m! I was to learn that in my area of Normandy, the jumps were always higher than the specifications, whereas in Paris they were sometimes lower. One had to ask where the horse had competed to understand its level.

I was so interested to see the type of horse one used in the speed class in France, as this was my favorite division at home. Standing near the gate, I heard, rather than saw, the approach of the first horse. With a thunder of noise, a huge heavy mare trotted into the ring with such an energy that the ground shook. My mouth was open! I could not imagine this to be in the speed class. Dorothy du Marais (which translates loosely to "Dorothy of the Swamp") flew around the course, ridden by Normandy rider Jean-Luc Dufour to an unbeatable time and to huge applause. A crowd favorite, Jean-Luc would become one of my best friends and advisors over time. The coliseum shook with the applause and the heavy gallop of the mare as she retired out into the darkness. I could not picture this mare in the speed classes at Wellington. She won the class, and I went away hoping to find horses of a more modern type to develop for the jumper divisions at home.

In time, Jean-Luc would become a forerunner in crossing his mares with German and Dutch stallions to improve the French breed without losing the character and the logic found in the Selle Français. Modern breeding in France produces winners in every part of the sport around the world.

I tried horses in all the remote areas of the country. My French was improving and I was able to see the country. I found areas where the horses tested positive for piroplasmosis and could not be exported. I found areas where horses were less expensive. I tried horses in any part of the sport in case they could be trained to jump.

One such horse, a five-year-old bay gelding, half Anglo, was supposedly intended for dressage. He was at a very low level of training, but nice. I rode for a few minutes before asking the owner if he could make me a little jump. *"Non!"* he cried. *"This horse is not to jump, never!"* He seemed very upset at the thought. He moved to the side of the ring to talk to a client arriving for a lesson, and I cantered over a pile of jump poles on the ground. Wow! He jumped beautifully! I turned and jumped it again. But, the owner saw me. *"Stop!"* he yelled. *"No jumping! Get off!"* I did. But I bought the horse. He became Inspector Gadget, a champion amateur event horse in America for Dr. Maria Brazil. He was phenomenal. Dr. Brazil went on to buy at least 10 horses from me, all successful in eventing and show jumping.

I decided to concentrate on my new way of earning a living and to temporarily put my first love of teaching to the side. I resigned from Marie Charlotte's training and began to travel the countryside. Many times, I was accompanied by friends looking for horses to take home for their clients.

♊

RIDING LESSON

The method of riding and training horses is more or less determined by the nature of the horse and his physical characteristics, plus the work for which he is intended. This has been true over time and has produced methods as diverse as the Weyrother method and the Caprilli method. The American, German, Hungarian, Portuguese, and French methods are all wonderful methods that work beautifully. A study of each of them is well justified as a basic education for a trainer. It takes time.

I was lucky to be a shy kid and not into social life. I read and read about these systems and had ideas about riding that I never would have had in the cornfields of Minnesota. I pursued my direction with the arrival of Karl Mikolka in my life, who taught the Weyrother method. Reiner Klimke, equally passionate about the classical methods, taught me his German method, and my eventual migration to France allowed a deep immersion into the French method. All classical methods work. The best method must be that which corresponds with the horse. There can be no strict adherence to a method that is not acceptable to the animal.

The French method is centered on lightness, freedom, and forward riding. It is closest to the American system where self-carriage is shown in every hunter competition. The light seat, the long neck, and the freedom of rein all correspond with a "blood" horse. One of the foundation breeds for the French was the Anglo-Arab. A very light horse, full of blood, highly sensitive, and intelligent, his influence in the later breeding of sport horses was invaluable. Another of these foundation breeds was the AQPS ("Other Than Thoroughbred"). This breed, still raced today, is

AN AMERICAN APPRECIATION OF THE FRENCH SYSTEM

comparable to the American "Seven Eighths Breed." He is close to a full blood but with something else.

These two breeds were, in my friend Jack Le Goff's opinion, the best breeds in the world for eventing. They are close in character and in physical attributes to the American Thoroughbred. As a result of this breeding, the French method evolved. The Thoroughbred was the horse available for the eventing and show jumping competitions in America. As a result of the breed, the American method evolved. It is interesting how the two methods share so many concepts.

But things changed. The Americans began to import German warmbloods. At the time the new European horse came on the scene in America, the breeding in Europe was a heavier, slower-thinking horse. This horse produced no adrenaline. He did not rise to the occasion like a blood horse will. He could be spooky. He was responsible for an evolution in the American scene, especially in dressage training. Because classical dressage was very rarely taught in the USA, trainers were rapidly imported. Some were fabulous, such as De Nemethy, Folteny, and Watjen. Others were not...

Absolutely frustrated by my inability to ride this new type of horse, I went to Germany to get help from Reiner Klimke. He let me ride his horses, which were hot. He told me that the good warmblood has energy and curiosity like any thoroughbred. He told me to make a better selection in Europe. I did.

At the same time, the regulations of the show jumping competitions were changing: shorter time allowed, flatter cups, and highly sophisticated course designers. The Northern European breeders rapidly changed their breeding to produce this faster, modern horse. The German method evolved to accommodate the new horse and the new structure of the competition. German riders started to ride more like American riders!

When I moved to France, the French competition had not yet evolved and the breeding was closed to outside influence. The program was, in my mind, stagnant. The changes effected in the breeding in France by forward-thinking breeders, and an opening up of the French National Stud, rapidly produced a new type of horse that was really competitive in both three-day eventing and show jumping.

When I had toured France earlier with Jack Le Goff to find horses for the U.S. team, I watched a lot of riding as we were shown hundreds of horses. In the car, I asked Jack why we saw so little evidence of the old classical French method of riding. He sighed and told me that it was a thing of the past and only to be seen at Saumur, where money was not an issue. The old breeds that he favored were not popular, and the ones bred in Normandy were too heavy. We did not go to Normandy at all.

It is a great regret that he was not able to see the transition to what is now the modern French horse bred in Normandy and elsewhere. The influx of blood coming from the inspired breeding in Germany, with the French, the natural galloper that he is, has produced a horse at the top in both disciplines!

The breeding of this horse has also produced a remarkable return to the classical French method of riding. Lightness, freedom, and forward riding are all to be seen again in France at top competitions. In the 2022 Top 10 competition in Geneva, three of the 10 qualified were French. Kevin Staut has become an icon of style and technique worldwide.

The method of riding and training horses must be the method that corresponds to the nature and physical characteristics of the horse. The rider who is open to his horse will learn from his horse. As an American living in France, I am doubly appreciative of the positive and correct evolution toward the classical method of French riding.

CHAPTER NINETEEN
HORSE DEALING 101

I had a lot to learn. My friends and fellow professionals from home learned with me because I dragged them on horse hunting trips all over Europe. I drove for days at top speed following German and French scouts to see what they had found. I developed a network of scouts to find and group together horses that suited whoever was with me.

Earlier in my life, I had been greatly helped in my horse hunting in France by UNIC, Union Interprofessionnelle du Cheval. UNIC, a government organization to assist foreign horse buyers in France with no commissions taken, was run at the time by my good friend Christian Meunier. Christian was a best friend of Jack Le Goff and had helped Jack find event horses many times. When I came to France to find horses before I became a resident, Christian would group horses for me to try. I bought five in one day from Yves Lemaire, leaving us enough time in my trip to go stag hunting with the Chardonnay. Christian's family home in the country was near his uncle's stag hunting pack and Christian was a Whip. We always found the time to hunt on my horse trips.

As I had only hunted the fox, stag hunting was new to me. The gamekeeper of the private forest selects the stag, usually an old stag, to be hunted and to be culled. In the morning, he goes with the huntsman and a small part of the pack to identify the hoofprint of that stag and its smell. Once the small pack of hounds is sure, they are stopped and the full pack is brought on. Then the field of riders is also allowed to come to the start. As the pack is released, the roar of the hounds in the forest is incredible!

At 11 a.m., one is at full speed, but in the trot, after the hounds in the forest. The breed of choice for the hunt is the French Trotter because of his stamina and his price. I tried, usually unsuccessfully, to force my trotter into the gallop, to save myself from the pounding of a trot too fast to post. Swerving left and right, I could sometimes get a gallop, but I unnerved my fellow riders. We trotted for hours on the lanes in the forest, sometimes crashing through the woods.

The stag must be taken. He is exhausted and would die of that, but it is the responsibility of the Hunt to take him. Because of this, the Hunt can last into the dark of night. Eventually, the stag will swim into a lake, a boat is thrown out, and the Whip goes out to kill the stag with a dagger. I was invited into the boat but demurred, saying that I could not swim. We would ride back to the truck, arriving late, ship home, and stiffen up into a form of rigor mortis by morning. I always hunted after the tryouts of horses were over.

As I lived in Virginia during some of the times that I went to France to buy horses, I invited Christian to hunt with the Piedmont Hunt in Middleburg. Our good friend Patrice Renaudin, Director of the French Breeders Association, came too, and we borrowed horses for my French friends from Foxcroft School. We also had the pleasure of Helie de Nouille in our French invasion, as Helie was on post at the French embassy in Washington.

Once, we were galloping down a long hill to jump a coop at the bottom when Christian pulled up beside me. *"What do we do at the bottom of the hill?"* he asked.

"Jump that coop!" I replied.

"I have never jumped!" he cried, as we neared the coop.

"Follow me, and lean forward," I yelled as my horse left the ground. I didn't look back, fearing the worst.

He galloped up beside me with a big grin and I knew he was hooked for life!

When I moved to France and organized horse hunting excursions for my friends, I tried to group horses as UNIC had done for me. This enabled us to see more horses and make better comparisons. My scouts in each area found good facilities and did the research on all the horses presented. It worked out very well, but I drove for hours. I learned a lot and heard a lot of life stories between stops.

I learned that Ralph Caristo refused to ride in a car going more than 200 km an hour (125 mph). I had to alert all my scouts to not drive so fast. When we drove into Switzerland, Ralph was obliged to drive, as I had lost my right to drive in that country due to excess speed. We went to visit Ralph and Holly's daughter Heather, who was riding at Gerhard Etter's stable in Müntschemier. This is a wonderful stable for young kids to try the horse life. Alumni include Henri Prudent, Peter Wylde, Elodie Frotiee and her sister Lea, and many other young professionals. In my memory, Ralph bought half the stable and became lifelong friends with Gerhard.

I learned that Brad Spragg could not be driven through a tunnel. All routes had to be planned with no tunnels. Not easy. He threatened to faint and/or vomit if he was taken into a tunnel. In a rainstorm, with the wipers at full speed, we hit a bird. The bird was big—a buzzard, I thought. He was killed instantly, but caught in the wiper. Brad was horrified, as was our other passenger, Mindy Darst, a well-known hunter and pony trainer from Ohio. Blood was spread and re-spread over the windshield as we arrived at our next stop to see horses. By then, we were all laughing hysterically. The stable owners received us in a reserved manner, which only set us off again. Luckily we found good horses and were able to buy something. Then we washed the car!

Mindy went on lots of these exhausting trips with me, buying many horses. At her Lochmoor Farm in Ohio, she trained hundreds of pony riders and handled lease contracts on many ponies and horses, as well as brokering sales. She was indefatigable. We tried horses in France until my scout was exhausted and sent us on our own at about 10:30 p.m. We arrived at a stable with a small wooden indoor arena and one single lamp hanging in the middle. I jumped the jump that we built under the lamp while Mindy filmed me galloping out of the darkness, over the jump, and back into the darkness.

We tried horses until 3 a.m. in Germany so that she could make her plane from Frankfurt at 10 a.m. the next morning. We stopped for a quick dinner at about 9 p.m. on one trip. Mindy had two or three glasses of wine as we were very cold. We got to our last stop at 11 p.m. and the temperature was at -9° Celsius. The walls of the indoor were covered with ice crystals and very shiny. I hoped the horse coming out would be a poor one and that Mindy would want to leave, but I knew I was in trouble when she said in a low voice, *"I feel like the ice queen."* Too much wine. She asked to ride the horse, which was not a horse I wished her to get on. Luckily, she only stayed on a short time before coming to her senses, and we left. On another trip, Mindy, her husband Greg, and I drove from Germany to Amsterdam to have dinner with Joe Norick. We then drove to Paris to catch the morning flight to Cleveland. I drove for hours.

Bobbie Reber always brought juniors to ride the horses as we looked. She kept us and the dealers in gales of laughter and made very good deals. As I was her translator, I was able to modify her choice of words successfully. Bobbie has an exceptional eye for a horse in rustic surroundings. I was forced to buy a bigger car to cope with the luggage and saddles purchased during these tours.

Jeff Gogul became well-known as a very good rider, and soon people would come with horses they wanted him to ride, even if not to buy. He is highly regarded in the east of France, but also in the southwest, where he purchased many young horses. We found a lot of less-known parts of France in which we discovered horses, including Wendy Lewis's amateur hunter, Forget Paris. We bought every horse we could from François's breeding program, and François came to the USA to study with Danny Robertshaw and Ron Danta. François wanted to develop the best hunters in France.

During the long drives with Jeff, I learned about all of his life as a kid learning to ride, and we were well amused by his stories and view of life. He likes antiques as well as I do, and we began to stop at antique stores along the way. Soon, the car was full of purchases.

Wendy Peralta also made a huge impression by riding so well during the trials of horses. The sellers really enjoyed having Wendy try their horses and suggest improvements. Wendy finally directed me toward some better hotels. I was always trying to save my clients money. At one hotel, a train passed by her window in the dead of night. She chose the hotels after that...

Noel Vanososte, who had been a working student in Virginia for two years, came to France often to buy horses for his huge group of students in Venezuela. He loved to buy from Laurent Guillet in the east of France, and never failed to amaze us by picking horses out of the group that went on to huge successes in South America. One of the horses he selected, Conrad, won the South American World Cup with Noel, and both the Central American and the Caribbean Individual Gold and Team Gold medals. I liked the horse well enough, but it became another horse with Noel. In the end, we flooded Venezuela with nice French horses. Laurent really does his homework and finds horses in every corner of France.

With my friends, I always had complete confidence. I made a big mistake when I was asked to accompany a group of riders from Turkey. They had asked for horses to jump big classes, 1.50m or more. They needed three horses. I made contacts and we began in France, then moved to Germany. We tried horses at all my friends, and they jumped the maximum with all the horses. When we arrived in Germany, we were taken to the stable where the then-coach of the Dutch squad, Bert Romp, was training. He was in the ring during the tryouts of the first two horses, and he approached me at the side of the ring.

"I want to warn you about these riders," he began. *"They were here two weeks ago with someone else to try horses too. They are not buyers, they are triers. They want to jump big jumps but have no opportunity at home so they book a buying tour with no intention of buying. This enables them to ride and to get a lot of advice, all free. Leave them at the hotel and stop the tour."*

I was forever grateful for his kindness, as he didn't know me. I had made a huge misjudgment. In the years to follow, this happened again with two groups from the Middle East and one young man from Venezuela, but I recognized the situation rapidly. I was helped by many other professionals along my way. It is the spirit in our sport and it must be protected and fostered by all. One of the best pieces of advice I was ever given was by an Irish trainer, Mike Burke, in Massachusetts. He told me that an association with a client may last only three years due to life changes. An association with a fellow professional can last 20 years or more. One should always look out for the fellow professionals in one's circle. It was great advice and affected my life in the right way. Bert Romp's advice was given in that spirit and saved me at that moment.

The work involved in exporting a horse does not stop once the horse is found. Bloodwork must be taken to determine that the horse is exportable to its destination. Then, a good vet must do a pre-purchase exam and send all the X-rays, with a report in English, to the buyer's vet. I use only one shipping agency, Equi-Services. The owner, Olivier Bossard, was a working student in Virginia and had formed his company on his return. He made a very wise choice in marrying Nathalie, who was already in the shipping industry and speaks many languages. With their help, my transport issues were handled perfectly. Still, I found a lot of paperwork waiting for me after each of these marathon horse-buying trips.

Although lucrative, dealing in horses was never my passion in life. Teaching and training horses are the first priorities on my list of preference, next comes competition, and then buying and selling. Selling to my students or ex-students to further their careers was a very satisfying compromise. I continued for years.

♊

RIDING LESSON

One of the most valued qualities in a sport horse is his natural balance. Volumes have been written about how to select a young horse with apparent balance, the conformation that lends itself to good balance, and how not to spoil the balance during the education of the horse. Still, there is more to be said.

A horse can be balanced when he is standing to be judged for conformation, but be unbalanced once he is in motion, once he carries a rider, or once he assumes the speed at which he will perform. The important factor of balance for a horse is his balance in motion and his balance with a rider.

The horse balances himself firstly with his neck. That is why contact with the rein too early in the training, which leads to a shortened neck or a horse that leans on the hand, can ruin his natural balance. I believe this premise to be universally accepted and I will not dwell on it.

The horse can also improve his balance by improving his stance on the ground. There are examples of this which will clarify how he does that:

1. The horse who does not balance well in transport is easily made calmer by giving him a double or triple space. This enables him to spread his legs apart. Improved stance.

2. The horse who is learning to put all his weight on his hind legs, such as in a levade, will spread his hind legs apart. Improved stance.

3. The cutting horse in front of his cow, prepared to go left or right in a hurry, spreads his front legs apart. Improved stance.

4. The horse at the takeoff for a tall jump will put both hind legs on the

NATURAL BALANCE

ground to push hard, but with a wider space between them than usual. Improved stance.

5. The horse in piaffe, but insecure, will sway left and right to improve his stability. Improved stance.

So there are two types of balance challenges: weight to the front and weight to the back, and, equally important but rarely discussed, weight to the left and right.

Walk on a fence or walk on a very thin line, and you will rapidly have a balance challenge. Walk on a broader track and you immediately feel secure and can go back to swinging your arms as you go. Horses which are stiff and inflexible in their chest and hip muscles can have difficulty balancing as they cannot improve their stance in motion.

At this time, it is important to return to the discussion of conformation, which pertains to balance. A very narrow horse was often described as having both front legs in the same bucket. This type of horse can have the described difficulty in balancing left and right. A very wide-shouldered and wide-hipped horse, although having a broad stance, is not the answer. He cannot canter well and is not fluid enough for the sport. The ideal conformation lies between these extremes, and the dressage and gymnastic training is the solution to any difficulty. It is said that one cannot teach balance. This is probably true. It is the simplest solution to buy a well-balanced horse.

However, a horse can have spoiled his natural balance due to poor training, and he can be reeducated to find it again. A horse can be a genius in one area and blocked in another. Correcting a problem in this second category of balance is easy and will have an immediate impact. It involves lateral work, either leg-yielding or shoulder-in, but not half pass or travers. The emphasis must be put upon the action of the outside front leg or the outside hind leg, instead of the habitual attention given to the inside front and hind. It is the distance between the legs that stretches the muscles and ligaments and loosens the horse. For example, in the right shoulder-in, the left shoulder and the left hind are more important in this aspect than the right shoulder and right hind.

The horse must be taught, slowly, kindly, and in the rhythm, to spread his legs apart. If he cannot do this, force is not the answer. Repetition with affection will loosen the frozen mechanism every time. Once the horse has been worked correctly for even a week or two, he will possess the key to his balance. He will become calmer, and his balance will enable him to be more confident.

A balanced horse is a joy to ride. Any rider will remark on a well-balanced horse. A balanced horse is secure on his feet and able to obey easily. This horse is calm and willing because of his balance. Volumes have been written. There is always more to say. There is always more to learn.

CHAPTER TWENTY
TIMEOUT TO FIND ROOTS

A wonderful coincidence changed my life. I needed a small house to rent in my favorite department of Calvados, not far from Deauville. I heard of a guest house and went to visit and meet the owners. I fell into a world apart from my own. The owner of the house was an Iranian who lived with his French wife, in exile, in Beuzeville. Their story unfolded to me gradually as I became their tenant, and then their driver (I could see that they needed one).

Ahmad Eghbal was the top diplomat of Iran under the shah, just before the revolution and the ensuing death of the shah. He was the Ambassador to the United States and created the Iranian Embassy in San Francisco. When the shah and his wife Farah toured the United States, Ahmad's wife, Zette, gave a seated dinner for the entourage at the embassy. She told me how she accomplished that and I learned a lot. It was hard to rapidly train the servers who knew little of the protocol of a state dinner. Not only were they to serve properly and clear each course with no plate touching another, but each server was meant to stand behind a guest, at attention, napkin folded over his arm, during the consumption of each course. In order to ensure that there was never the clink of dishes colliding, there were napkins between each plate at all times.

It was also difficult to find matching service, silver, and glassware corresponding to each wine at the time in San Francisco. Zette approached the best hotels in the end. Each course was served on matching plates, but no two courses were on like porcelain. There were 40 seated diners at the event. Every wall sconce was changed to a candle and flowers for the evening. Candles were changed by the servers as needed.

The huge affair was a success and Zette had a breath of relief as the shah left on his return to an unhappy Iran. Ahmad's brother was the prime minister. When the shah finally died, still unwilling to see that popular feeling was against him, Ahmad's brother also died. The revolution took its toll.

They told me of their experience during the fall of the shah. Ahmad was then the Ambassador to The Hague. They were living in a lovely house with a huge atrium for Zette's parrot, a lifelong pet. Ahmad and Zette were at breakfast, parrot flying loose around them, when all of the eight doors into the atrium flew open at the same time. Armed Iranian guards ran into the room, one of them killing the parrot right away, yelling, *"Don't move! Stand up, but don't move!"*

Ahmad and Zette were to be transported back to Iran as part of the overthrow of the government. They were terrified. Meanwhile, one of the maids had called the Dutch police as soon as she saw what was happening. They arrived, rescued Ahmad and Zette, and, as Zette was a French citizen, set them on a train to Paris. Zette's mother received them, sold her enormous house near Paris, and helped to find the isolated house with a guest house in Normandy. There, they lived in exile, hoping never to be found. Ahmad could never go home to find his family or retrieve his belongings.

My great fortune was to hear their stories. Ahmad told me of being educated by an American couple at the American School in Tehran. I had never heard of that school. He told me of the village his father owned and how the women walked seven miles to get the water, how the fires under the baths were lit at 4 a.m. for bathing before prayers, and that electricity came to the village in 1981. I never knew these things. He told me of the telephone being located in the Post Office in each town. Iran was rich, but the people were deprived.

Zette told me of the German occupation of France in the Second World War, and how her first husband, a member of the resistance, was captured in Paris and taken to a concentration camp. Her mother fled to the south to hide. Zette remained in Paris with her father, who had a large hôtel particulier, also known as a grand townhouse, and a very good chef. Zette learned to cook. Her husband returned, having lost his mind at the end of the war. The marriage was ended. I had never heard these things. Ahmad and Zette met at the embassy, Ahmad having entered the diplomatic corps and Zette being on her father's arm at a function. In the end, they married.

Had I never moved to France, I would never have heard their story. I would never have read the books in Ahmad's library that told of the terrible mistakes England and the United States made in the Middle East concerning oil. I would never have met all those Middle Eastern exiles in Nice, where they gave a huge dinner in honor of Ambassador Eghbal. I heard stories of unimaginable escapes. I met women who had walked across continents to escape tyranny, coming from important families who had lost favor. These brave women remade their lives in new countries, like France or America, when they finally arrived. Nice holds a community of these brave people, living out their life in exile. I was glad to drive my friends as they were elderly and I learned a lot.

I would never have learned the cooking secrets of Zette, the stories of life during the war, and her terrible time in Iran when Ahmad was recalled for a time between posts. I would never have learned that they dined often with Josip Tito while on post there in Yugoslavia. I would never have known that Tito predicted the awful breakdown of his country at his demise. He told Ahmad that it broke his heart to know in advance what was to come and to be powerless to stop it. In fact, it was a terrible revolution, as predicted, with thousands killed and tortured.

While I lived with Ahmad and Zette, my life with horses was diminished slightly to privilege what I was learning. Americans are taught a rather patriotic view of history at best. Ahmad was very pro-American due to his education at the American School, but he was a clear-sighted historian, having lived it. His dream was to live long enough to see the people of Iran finally overthrow the mullahs who govern the country under strict religious law. He did not succeed in that, nor did he ever succeed in returning to his country, for fear of losing his life. Americans know nothing of exile.

I realized that my move to France was one of the best ideas of my life. I was able to see and understand a lot more of the world. I rented their little guest house for three years until I saw a property I just had to buy. While hiking one day near Bourgeauville, on the well-marked trails around the stud farms there, I passed a little house in bad shape on the side of a hill. There were two outbuildings with it and a stream at the bottom of the hill. Bathed in sunshine, it was a peaceful view, and I stood awhile to enjoy it.

The very next day, the realtor, who was looking for a small property for me, called. *"I have found a small house for you. But the ceilings are so low that you may not be able to stand up."*

I asked her where the house was located and she told me Bourgeauville. I was happy to go to see it, after my hiking in that area the previous day. Imagine my surprise when I realized, approaching the same house on its proper driveway, that I was back at the same view!

The house was indeed very low, but the elderly couple inside were very small. There was no heat other than the fireplace. It was tiny, with the bedroom upstairs under the roof. The grounds were covered with brambles and brush, but there were about 10 acres and a lovely stream. The couple was tired of building the fire, fighting the dirt driveway, and the approach of the ever-expanding brambles. They wanted to sell. It was a mess, but I bought it, seeing great promise in the location. I soon discovered it was the project of my life.

I arranged to have the house taken down and rebuilt, adding two meters of height. I was not allowed, by the mayor, to enlarge the footprint of the house due to restrictions. This work took almost three years, as the French were working only 35 hours a week at the time. I used the three years to clear the land and see what I had purchased.

I bought a scythe. And a wheelbarrow. And I bought heavy gloves to protect my hands from thorns. I went to work, cutting down brambles at the southeast corner of the property. I began to uncover apple trees, holly trees, and pear trees. An old orchard!

Asking around the village for a man to advise me on trimming the fruit trees, I was told that I needed a pro. Soon word had spread and one day, I was approached by a pro while I was riding my horse at Haras de Chesnaye, where I kept my five horses. I put the horse in the stable and drove the pro, Emmanuel Lamotte, to see my project. As we came into the driveway, he saw my scythe on the ground beside my wheelbarrow.

"Stop," he said. *"What is that?"*

"My worksite!" I replied, with a sense of pride in the 15 meters that I had cleared.

He looked at me with an incredulous expression for a moment. *"Madame, at that rate you will never clear the land before the brambles have recovered this space. You need someone with equipment!"*

At the end of the tour that I gave Emmanuel, he had agreed to trim the trees and then begin to clear the land one and a half days each week. I was saved! We made lots of discoveries as we cleared the land. One day, Emmanuel came to find me, where I was planting a small flower garden, to say that he had made an important find. At the very entry onto my property, the stream divided in two. It became one stream again where it left my land. There was an island between the streams. When we finished clearing this big island, it became a wonderful place to plant anything that likes a humid ground. With the hill above and the island below, I had a place to plant any type of tree or bush that I liked.

Emmanuel was a gifted gardener and he had a very good imagination in creating all sorts of vegetable and flower gardens, as well as picking the right trees to set in. By the time the house was finished, I had a park to take care of. As I am a vegetarian, I ate what I grew. I could spend mornings on horses and afternoons on gardening!

We bought 200 railroad ties at a sale, intentionally not of the best quality. The best quality railroad tie is straight, square, and uninteresting. I wanted the ones that had a bend or a curve. We used them as stairs going up the hill, bridges across the stream, framing around gardens, and terracing the hill in some places. Placing them on the hill took ropes, the tractor, and a lot of bad language on Emmanuel's part. He often said that he would never work for an American again. But he stayed.

I rebuilt the smaller of the two timbered outbuildings into a summer kitchen. It was a magical place, with a big fireplace for cooking and a tiny makeshift kitchen for cleaning up. We took out everything between the timbers so that it felt more like outdoors than in. It was used a lot for dinners all summer long. I used a wheelbarrow to bring all the settings down the hill from the house before the guests arrived.

The larger outbuilding was on the higher place on the hill. I was unhappy about its imposing look. We decided to make a bank on the high side of the building and to plant poplar trees on top of the bank. This would overshadow the building and diminish its authority. I bought 12 very tall poplars, and Emmanuel almost quit!

"How do you think we can plant a 15-foot tree on top of a 4-foot high bank without a big tractor with a bucket lift?"

I told him that I thought our little and old machine would do it eventually, with help from wires to stabilize the new trees. We got them all up after more bad language. There were wires attached to posts everywhere. Three days later, in a big storm, at least half the trees fell. I dreaded calling Emmanuel with the news and I got the reaction I feared. However, he came over, and we got them all back up again.

By the time I moved into the house, it was surrounded by a magical garden park which took all my spare time to mow, weed, and trim. Even with Emmanuel's help one day each week, it was a lot of work. I loved it, but could only work half the day with horses, leaving time to keep my garden in shape. I was so happy to be the owner of my home again and not a renter. For the first time since I moved to France, I felt at home.

I was saddened by not being able to share the finished project with Zette, as she passed away during my first year of ownership. She loved the project. Ahmad followed her within a year, but he gave me three white birch trees to plant on the hill and was always happy to receive raspberries from the garden.

Chapter Twenty

CHAPTER TWENTY-ONE
MIXING FRANCE AND FLORIDA

At this time, I had sold most of my horses, my broodmare was retired, and the young horses were ridden at shows by Jean-Luc Dufour. I was hoping to keep my riding condition, so I approached my neighbor, Christian Hermon, who was the French agent for the wonderful horses being bred by Alfonso Romo in Monterrey, Mexico. The La Silla horses, using the name of the stud in Mexico, were sent to Christian for development and eventual sale in France. They were picked by Christian on his trips to visit Mr. Romo. Many were stallions, handled quietly and brought along with the minimum of stress.

When I asked Christian if I could come and ride every morning to keep my condition, he agreed very kindly. I did this every day within one kilometer of my home. Most of the time, I rode one a day, sometimes two. Sometimes, I kept one of my own at the stable to also ride. It was a great atmosphere for horses with no stress. When I had students at the house, Christian generously allowed me to teach them on his nicest horses, giving a boost to the young riders in our area. Alexandre Dufour, whose parents are top breeders in Normandy, rode at the stable, as did Mathis Burnouf, who later rode for Kevin Staut and others with great success. It was a huge advantage for these juniors to see how Christian, a world-class rider, ran his sales yard with no stress and no lack of empathy for the horse.

Sometimes, I helped Christian's rider, Delphine Perez, who rode the horses with Christian at the shows. Delphine has a special gift of giving confidence to a young horse. One stallion that she was riding while I was at the stable was Vagabond de la Pomme.

Vagabond was a special horse. He had a naturally enormous stride, and at four and five was too young to be collected. Christian and Delphine had rightly decided to let the colt finish his younger years in a completely natural manner. As a six-year-old, he often left out a stride in lines of seven or more strides, but handled the combinations fine. He had a great year, spending more days hacking out on the roads than drilling in the ring, and he ended up looking very promising in the Young Horse Finals in Fontainebleau. It was time to start another phase of his education, and as he was sold, his new rider would have that project. The new rider was Pénélope Leprevost, who rode for Haras de Clarbec at the time. It was a project and took some time, but Vagabond was to learn to shorten his stride. It never became his favorite idea. Delphine had done a great job with this stallion.

During this period, I spent my winters in Wellington at the shows, coaching and visiting friends. Sometimes, I took my French students to visit and to see the show. I was constantly struggling to find housing for them during the busy circuit, but my friends came through. Betsy Geary, who trained for Marsha Dammerman at Sand Castle Farm in Grand Prix Village, was a long-time friend of mine from upper New York where we showed together. I could keep my horses there and sometimes use one of the condominiums.

Barbara Miles, also my close friend, who owned a farm in Loxahatchee, was very generous in housing both me and the kids I brought. Barbara, a lifelong friend, had helped me several times when I was broken by coming to Middleburg to ride and help me. Dr. Allen Leslie, a well-known vet at many of the international competitions, housed Mathis Burnouf. Dressage rider Valerie Haskell housed Lea Frotiee, who is now an upcoming professional in France. Alexandre Dufour, Elodie Frotiee, and other French juniors were welcomed by friends and came home with an expanded vision of the industry there. I took them to Dunkin' Donuts, Walmart, Motor Home Village, and Costco. Americana!

They were invited to Sand Castle's table by Betsy and Marsha, to watch the big night classes and have dinner with all the owners and riders. It was as much fun for me as it was for them. Katie and Henri Prudent invited all the Frenchies to their nearby farm and Katie gave lessons to a few. Olympic Silver medalist Chris Kappler gave them demonstration rides. Mindy Darst loaned a nice horse to Émilie Laporte to compete in the hunter class. All of the juniors that went with me to Wellington are now professionals in the sport.

I even took my blacksmith, Raphael Giret, to Wellington so that he could meet every North American blacksmith of the highest quality, all in one place. There were seminars, blacksmith shops, and new techniques. Raffi was in heaven! He is a great blacksmith and I was lucky that he did not move to Canada after that even though that was his longtime dream. I found that Wellington had evolved into an industry rather than a sporting event. The level of competition was world class and the money offered was fabulous. The number of sales and possibilities for clients was incomparable with other wintertime venues. But the horses did not live a life that was pleasant.

Other than those horses living on the nearby farms, the horses lived with no paddock and a small stall. Working areas were limited because of the show schedule. Trail riding was available and that was a saving grace. Horses were competed and used for lessons, and sometimes tried out on the same day to be sold. All my working students loved the excitement and the glamor of riding and watching the world's great riders perform in Wellington. I tried to get every student to Wellington to see it all. After 30 years of showing in Florida over the winters, I had watched the development of this show facility change from a reclaimed swamp to the world-class competition that it has become.

In order to accomplish this reclamation of land from the vast Florida wetlands, many lagoons and canals were dug to accommodate the water, and the surrounding land was elevated to rise above the water table. It was an engineering feat, which produced the land for the competition, as well as for the small private farms built all around the show. It was the first of its type in the world and raised the stature of Wellington to an international destination. It left the huge population of alligators in the area homeless and unhappy.

It took a long time for the horse show fans and participants to adapt to the roaming of the South Florida alligator, as he searched for a compromise with his former life of dominance. No body of water is too small to entice an alligator, if only for the night. The lagoon beside the De Nemethy ring was no exception, and alligators were seen watching the classes from the banks. After an unhappy ending for many Jack Russells, dog owners took the leash law much more seriously than previously. Alligators that appear to be sleeping are often watching their approaching prey, and they are remarkably fast for a short distance. Alligators grow forever, it seems, as they have reached extreme sizes.

The distance between the rings and the very furthest stalls became longer and longer as the show grew. One year, my stalls were one kilometer from the ring where I finished at dark. I led my horse back to the stalls, and unsaddled him in front of the tack room, setting the saddle on the ground. As I walked away to lead the horse to his stall, I heard a commotion in the dark tack room. After the horse was in his stall, I started the car and shone the headlights into the tack room. I had dodged a bullet, as there was a small two-meter alligator in the tack room! I went to the stable office, complained about the lack of lighting, and asked for help. The game department came, transported the young alligator away, and I cleaned my tack around midnight. The game department plays a big role in the horse show scene in Wellington. Theoretically, the captured alligators are relocated in the Everglades, but some are probably made into stew or shoes. One asks few questions in Florida about these things.

I love the countryside around Ocala, further north in Florida. I always tried to show in this area for at least half the winter, enjoying the Thoroughbred farms, the breeze-up sales, and the farms to rent during the show. I also love country music. In the past, the competition was of a lower level, less money was offered to the winners, and it was less expensive for the owners than it was in Wellington. Three hours north of Wellington, it was easy to do some of each. I could afford to bring extra horses to prepare for the spring and extra students to show in small classes. It was colder, but not winter, and lots of event riders, as well as show jumping enthusiasts, wintered in Ocala. The life for horses was more natural and that appealed to me.

Ocala has grown. I was not the only one to appreciate the advantages. The new extravagant World Equestrian Center will change Ocala into another version of Wellington. With the advantage of the existing farm country, and with the absence of alligators, pythons, and tropical skin problems, one can hope that the life of the horse can be better sustained in this area. The new facility is unequaled in the world. The horse industry is expanding constantly. The business opportunities in both real estate and horse sales are attracting non-horse people into the field. The danger to the animal is apparent. The preservation of the sport, the art of horsemanship, and the traditions surrounding the horse is the greatest challenge of the next generation. Much has been gained financially, with much being lost at the same time. When the influence of money invades a sport, or an art, there needs to be a strong presence of traditionalists to balance the outcome.

Jack Le Goff, Karl Mikolka, Alois Podhajsky, Bert de Nemethy, and others of this generation were traditionalists. Sadly, they are missing. The safekeeping of their spirit and love for the horse is the key to the future of our sport. The records set, the money made, and the prizes won will be forgotten, but the traditions should live on. The next generation must accept this challenge.

Young riders with traditional values are formed by mentors. A mentor is more than a teacher because of a closer relationship with his protégé than between a teacher and his many students. A protégé is more than a student because he is destined to mirror his mentor and to carry on his work. A mentor and his protégé spend much more time together than a teacher who teaches his student for an hour at a time. A mentor gives his life to his protégé. A protégé gives his future to his mentor.

I was present at one of the first North American Riders Group (NARG) meetings, when Chris Kappler, Olympic Silver medalist, spoke about the cost of taking students who could not afford to pay. He spoke of the rising price of competition as one of the real problems in helping young people who are not wealthy into the sport. The cost of competing has doubled since his talk. When a mentor spends his life with his protégé, hourly pay is forgotten. A working student is more likely to carry on traditions in the horse world than an hourly lesson student because of the time spent and the quality of the time spent with the professor. My working students led my life. I believe that the legacy of a teacher is in his protégés.

The Safe Sport Program, although probably not a bad idea entirely, rules out the mentor-protégé relationship altogether. A teacher is not allowed the proximity and presence in the life of a junior. One-on-one contact is to be strictly avoided. Inviting a close and confidential relationship with a student is considered dangerous and leads to possible abuse. I could not do today what I did in the past with my students. My greatest joy in life would never have happened. I also could not have been privileged in the way that I was by Mr. Roberts, who devoted his life to me and my riding. There were no ulterior motives in Mr. Roberts.

The traditions and interpretations that I have left with my protégés do not compare with the greats before me, but it is my contribution. I am sorry that this poorly interpreted program will probably make it impossible to be a mentor in many sports. This is what inevitably happens when one tries to legislate morality. The side effects of this program are catastrophic to the art of horsemanship, which can only be passed on from mentor to protégé.

Each year, when I came home from Wellington to a simpler life in Normandy, I felt a relief for the way that young horses are handled and the way that older horses live in real life, in this country where the animal comes first.

Ⅱ

RIDING LESSON

Communication with a horse by his rider is largely accomplished by touch. The contact between the hand of the rider and the mouth of the horse is a direct line of communication. Although much can be said about the various types of bits and nosebands in modern use to facilitate the rider's ability to establish a contact, the reality is that the horse must seek the connection. When it is the rider that takes the contact with the mouth, the problems of the horse being behind the vertical, the tongue being badly positioned in the mouth or out of the mouth, and the horse distorting his gaits or his frame in order to evade all become apparent.

It is not difficult, at a young age, to teach the horse to reach for the contact with the hand of the rider. It is extremely difficult to retrain a horse who has learned to evade contact by one of the forgoing escapes. The proper beginning pays off in the end.

Having established that the horse must reach for the connection, it is then a question frequently asked: How strong a contact is required to ensure that the horse is connected? The answer is not simple. The degree of pressure should always be as light as possible so as not to inhibit freedom, movement, or the fragile balance of the animal. To this end, one learns the value of the half-halt, the small vibrations, and a hand that is "alive" rather than completely still, all of which discourage a heavy connection.

The better the intellectual bond between horse and rider, the lighter may be the contact. At the level of Grand Prix in dressage, the rider can do a part of the test with the reins in one hand, for example. The little girl with her pony proudly jumps the course with no bridle. At the level of World

COMMUNICATION WITH A HORSE BY HIS RIDER

Cup show jumping, the horse may have no contact with the rein during the last stride before takeoff. These moments are proof of a horse and rider who think alike, as a result of previous experiences, probably with a firmer connection. The real goal of all training is not to have a stronger contact with the mouth. It is to have a lighter contact with the mouth.

Once a horse can balance with a rider, and only then, one establishes a connection between the hand and mouth by teaching the horse to reach for the contact. This is easiest to do on the ground, and anyone can learn to do it. The degree of desired contact is relative to the work that the horse is learning: a steadier hand for a nervous, flighty, or less focused horse, and less contact for a poorly balanced one. One great danger, other than those listed above, of too much contact too soon in the life of the horse is that the horse may use the hand as a "fifth leg" and lean on that. Loss of self-carriage due to a heavy hand is a classic and debilitating problem.

One of the very best concepts of the French school of riding is the idea that the contact with the outside rein should always be more than the contact with the inner rein. The horse can be completely controlled by the outside rein and the inside leg, leaving him with more freedom and more self-carriage than a horse equally on both hands. Certainly, and undeniably, a horse with more connection on the inner rein than the outer rein will be off-balance and constrained.

The moments of complete freedom from contact are rewards given to the horse to motivate him towards good behavior and interpretive thinking. Therefore, one must keep as the main goal the eventual freedom of the horse. The main goal is not to dominate or to subjugate the horse until he accepts losing his freedom. This will always produce a dull horse with no initiative.

Reiner Klimke held the belief that any horse that was not lame could be trained to do the Grand Prix in dressage. He said that the real point was to train the horse to that highest level without losing the spark and initiative of the young horse. Domination and subjection were never part of his method. Lightness was foremost in his estimation.

Self-carriage was always extremely important to Karl Mikolka in his training. He had many skillful techniques, such as well-timed half-halts and transitions within and in between paces, to avoid inadvertently encouraging the horse to lean on the rein. Once the horse has learned to use the rein as a support, his potential as an athlete has been diminished. Lightness was his objective at every stage.

The high-level show jumper is not different from the high-level dressage horse in that initiative and interpretive behavior will always benefit the eventual performance. The contact between the rider's hand and the mouth of the horse is a line of communication that permits the rider to direct, alert, calm, and interpret his horse. This same line of communication allows the horse to interpret his rider. As the two work together over time, lighter contact is always the goal, with more freedom permitting the horse to work easily and with less stress.

CHAPTER TWENTY-TWO
ENTER KEVIN STAUT

When Delphine left the stable of Christian Hermon to take a very good position as the young horse trainer at Haras de Coudrette, I was pleased for her but sad for the young horses she left behind. At Haras de Coudrette, the breeding of show horses was the priority. Madame Emmanuel Perron-Pette was the owner and director, and she had a dream. Delphine was to handle the initial training and competitions of the young horses at the home farm.

At the Haras de la Forge, created by Perron-Pete, the dream was to be fulfilled. Huge installations for training, including an indoor arena, a large grass field, and a large all-weather surface, were built beside a stable with three separate wings. Each wing was a center aisle barn with boxes of huge dimensions for twelve horses. Each aisle had its own large tack room, lounge, and wash stalls. Between the aisles were feed rooms, a pharmacy, a blacksmith area, and a veterinarian position. Upstairs was a lounge for all and viewing of the work in the indoor.

There was an all-weather track around the complex and plenty of paddocks, a longe pen, and a walker. There were numerous apartments, housing for grooms, and a lovely manor house for the owners. One of the small houses had been made into an office. There was nothing left out! Three riders were installed at the Haras, to be sponsored in the direction of the highest competition on horses bought or bred by Perron-Pete. These riders were Kevin Staut, Patrice Delaveau, and Franck Schillewaert. At the onset, it was planned that Franck would handle the seven- and eight-year-olds, and Kevin and Patrice would ride at the top shows. It was all for the benefit of the French team and the sport.

Delphine suggested to Kevin and Emmanuel that I would be a good addition to the program. Kevin has an insatiable appetite for learning and he was fascinated by the American system. We had meetings and I agreed to come to La Forge two days every week to collaborate with Kevin on his horses. I was thrilled. I was to continue with Delphine as well and her young horses at Haras de Coudrette. I had a big schedule, and it was in my preferred activity of teaching and training. I immediately abandoned the activity involving the sales of horses. I began right away and the first horse that I rode, to make a demonstration of the half-halt, was Reveur. He was unfamiliar with this aid and I was surprised to find this. Kevin remounted, tried the new control, and said, "That is really interesting." I noticed that he could watch and copy, exactly as I had taught my students years ago. He did exactly as I had done, with exactly the same result.

I rode Reveur a lot, and the two of us came, eventually, to an understanding. Reveur had decided that he knew it all, and was pretty stuck in his unwillingness to learn. I decided to teach him something completely new to freshen his mind and to help him improve his downhill balance. The perfect movement would be a pirouette! He had to bend his hind legs and lift his forehand to do this, and I was sure that it would help his jump. At first, he was uninterested and unhappy with me, but Reveur is very smart and can learn anything quickly once he opens his mind. The first good pirouette that he made was his third attempt after all the preliminary preparations. That was pretty quick! I had to laugh at him after that. He was like a dog with a new toy! He could go twice around very soon and his expression was completely changed. He was, during the pirouette, completely light in his mouth. Also, he understood. He thought it was a game! I knew how to train this one.

The next thing that happened gave me a window into Kevin. At about 6.30 a.m., my phone rang. I saw that it was Kevin.

"Is anything wrong? Why are you calling me this early? Aren't you at Helsinki?"

"Yes, I am," he replied. *"I am in the schooling area riding before the show, and I just did my first pirouette!"*

He had watched and decided to try it. Reveur was an expert and Kevin could feel the point of doing pirouettes with a jumper. I realized that this rider had an open mind and would use new methods that worked for him. I knew how to help this rider.

At the time I met Reveur, he was only alive and enthusiastic when jumping. During flatwork, he was low and heavy, and slow and uninterested. One cannot improve the horse in that mood. His enjoyment of learning the pirouette encouraged me to teach him middle trot, and then the departure into middle trot from the halt. This he found very interesting and fun. He anticipated the depart and his enthusiasm created a new horse. I worked on his flying change, which had always been lackluster. The first good one that he gave me was followed by a buck which I rewarded. That flying change led to others that were good, and the ensuing canter was more fun to ride.

It amazed me to hear the speakers on Equidia, the National Horse Channel on French television, begin to comment on Reveur's changed balance. I was unaccustomed to hearing speakers who knew what they were watching and who voiced their opinions. Here were horsemen in the media! And they were speaking to an educated public. I was thrilled.

Reveur loved to buck in joy. I have always felt that rolling over from side to side and full bucking are great ways to loosen up the back. Years earlier, in Germany, Reiner Klimke had asked me to ride Sekur, his wife Ruth's horse, out on the track around the farm in order that the horse could buck. He said I was afraid of nothing and that the horse needed to do this. I let him buck his way around twice, and Reiner thanked me profusely. Reveur liked to buck on the longe. We had perfect footing and I am good with a longe, so I let him do this just before he left for the 2016 Olympics in Rio. I made the groom mad but our horse left in fine spirits. He was, as the Irish fellows say, "full of himself."

Boosting the morale is a key concept of mine in training a jumper. A horse needs initiative and a positive outlook to jump. There is no possibility of forcing a horse, as a long-term method, to compete. His rider can advise; the horse must perform. Reiner Klimke was right when he told me that one of his greatest achievements was to train Ahlerich to the highest level without losing his "joie de vivre." Ahlerich had a huge character and was very hot. It was not the same as Reveur, but it was exactly the same challenge.

Jack Le Goff was a master in developing a "will to win" in both his horses and his riders. The importance of morale in a competitor is as important as any of the other facets, such as education, condition, experience, and talent. With Reveur, I felt my most important contribution to his performance in Rio would be in his morale. Kevin did a fantastic job, as always, under huge pressure. The French team won the gold medal in Rio.

I rode some wonderful horses during our years at Haras de La Forge with which Kevin competed all around the world. There were no two alike but Kevin won with them all. He did a great job for his sponsor but it was an aging group and the end was in sight. The sport has enlarged to the point where a rider needs six or more horses to jump the 1.60m classes in order to remain on the scene. The Nations Cup Series necessitates a different horse from the World Cup competition. The Global Champions Tour is another series of prestigious competitions in important and faraway venues. We used a lot of horses and the plane schedule was impressive.

Kevin returned from the show every week on Sunday evening if possible. He prepared the horses to leave on Tuesday or Wednesday, by riding them on Sunday evening, and Monday and Tuesday when possible. The horses from the competition just ended usually arrived at home Monday night or Tuesday. Usually, Kevin left again on Wednesday. My job was at home, and there were usually young riders as well as me to ride the 10 horses at home. Horses could go out three times a day, on the walker, in a training session, and on the beach. Condition is a huge factor in soundness, and we had an older group. They were very fit and rarely missed a day, even days when they shipped. Kevin rode the horses very early in the morning the same day that they were to ship. Horses worked the day after their arrival from competition, as if they had not been away. No details were left to chance.

For Joy was the last horse to be retired, and he was a survivor. Riding For Joy was a little like riding a squirrel. He was a fast-thinking horse with a huge sense of humor. The trick was to establish a steady connection so that his thought process could be more controlled. However, he was very crafty and did not like to be connected. He would very sneakily leave the contact on one side or another, and then spin or step to the side or shy at nothing. Games! He made me laugh, and his agility and fast thinking were what kept him in form longer than any of the others. Delphine told me that before he was castrated at five, he was just impossible. After that, he was funny and hard to channel but a winner when he concentrated.

Ayade was always one of my favorite mares. She was initially hard to mount, but with carrots and some tack changes this disappeared and I rode her a lot. She was extremely smart and tried to do anything asked of her. Sometimes, she filled in for other horses by jumping classes higher than she was intended to jump, and always tried her maximum. She went on to do what I considered her life calling: being a great young rider horse for Valentine Delaveau, under the watchful eyes of her father Patrice. They did a great job in lowering the pressure from the big classes for this very careful mare. She will be a wonderful broodmare now.

I learned that Patrice was not only one of the fastest riders in the world but was equally fast with his wit. It was fun for me to ride in the same ring as Patrice and Kevin for the years we spent at La Forge. When "the page turned" and the horses became too old, Patrice took on the horses to finish their careers. Kevin decided to move to his family farm in Pennedepie to continue under his own roof, while Patrice carried on at La Forge. We had been privileged with the wonderful facility created by Emmanuel Perron-Pette. It was fun to have Patrice and Kevin and all the young assistant riders for company and feedback. The level of riding was very high, but never stressful, and always positive for the horses. We had worked many wonderful horses.

RIDING LESSON

I've spent my whole life with horses, and one aspect about being with horses that I really love is training the horse. Training horses has several challenges attached to it. One is that there are no two alike. That I think everyone knows, but the other very important aspect of training horses is that they many times are not cut out to do the same discipline. You might have a chosen field in mind for a horse, and it turns out later that it is not the right field for that horse. So you have to remain alert during the time you do the basic foundation of educating the horse at the beginning.

Karl Mikolka, coming from the Spanish Riding School, used our Friars Gate Farm in Pembroke, Massachusetts, as his dressage base. Karl did not have a bedside manner, and many times he would yell out things into the air, and we were expected to take them in. One morning, he arrived as 20 horses were working in the ring at the same time, and he yelled out into the open air, "Every horse deserves a life." Well, there was silence in the indoor arena for about 50 seconds while we assimilated that knowledge. I had no idea what he meant by that, but I just knew we were supposed to take this in. Whether it affected me or not, I was going to remember it.

At that time, I had a horse named Oliver. Oliver was a school horse. He was really good at walk and trot, but cantering was just beyond him. If you forced him to canter, he would be extremely nervous and the canter was not good at all. Cantering was out of Oliver's league. He was a walk-trot horse. So I used him only at the walk and trot. I taught people to post on Oliver; he was good at that. He also had a problem with things on the

TRAINING THE HORSE TO HIS PERSONAL BEST

ground: rails, puddles, a shadow, or anything on the ground could cause him to dissolve into a fit of nervousness. Now, I realize he was probably vision-impaired, but at that point, I didn't realize that. I just didn't face him with anything he didn't like. One day, I finished my lesson with Oliver, and Karl finished his lesson with a dressage rider at the same time.

He walked over to me and he said again, *"Every horse deserves a life."*

And I said, *"Yes, I have heard that, Karl, and I understand it."*

He said, *"I will take Oliver."*

I said, *"Really? What will you do with him? You're taking him away?"*

He said, *"I will take him to the dressage barn."*

The little girl who was riding Oliver got off; she was a little nervous about Karl. Karl took the horse and walked to the dressage barn with him. I didn't see Oliver for about two weeks; I was pretty busy. Karl was not there while I was there. It was not until about three weeks later that I saw Karl working Oliver in hand along the wall of the indoor arena.

Oliver had a square dressage pad and four white bandages on him. He had one of the expensive dressage bridles on, and Karl was treating him as though he was a champion. He taught Oliver how to do the levade. The levade is something like a rear, but the horse crouches down very low to the ground with intense flexion of his hocks. It is done, to Oliver's great relief, at the halt. Oliver did not need to move; he simply crouched in a rear-like position and stayed there, and he loved it. And Karl fed him carrots for this. Once Karl had taught him how to do levade, he took every single student that I had between the ages of 10 and 13. Every child in the stable was allowed to sit on Oliver while he did the levade. So these very young children were doing airs above the ground with no stirrups. They were doing the levade on Oliver.

Oliver got his picture in the yearbook. He was part of the yearly demonstration that we did to duplicate the Spanish Riding School's Sunday performance. We did it with children. Oliver did the levade between the pillars that were erected at X. He became famous. Everyone fed him carrots and visited him. He was at the peak of his career.

Every horse deserves a life.

That taught me a lesson, because Karl came from the academia of the Spanish Riding School, where there was no specific agenda in training a horse. There were no commissions to be made, no horses to be sold, no competition, and no prizes to be won. There was no other incentive to train the horses than to reach the top personal potential of every horse that was trained. That is pure training of horses. I always loved that. I realized that when you begin to train a horse and you teach them the basic rudimentary foundation of training, you must at the same time be on the watch for the tendency of that horse towards a certain discipline. When you find it, you must go in that direction. It has nothing to do with what you had planned for that horse; it has to do with the horse and where his tendencies lie.

I have another story to tell you about one of my favorite students of all time, Jan O'Donnell. She was a very well-known and good amateur hunter rider. Throughout her time with me from when she was 10 on a pony, then on an equitation horse, then on a junior hunter, and then an amateur hunter, she was always a good rider and a good student. One day, as an older teenager, she said to me, *"I would like to train my own horse. I would like to buy a young horse and train it."*

"Fine," I said. We found a Quarter Horse, an adorable little Quarter Horse with a dish face and a big tail. He was a bright chestnut and he had a very cute expression. Jan set out to train the horse.

Gradually, she taught him to do flying changes, which were easy; he did them automatically. He was very well-balanced and she taught him all the basics. But there was a problem. He jumped everything he was asked to jump, but he did not have a good style and there was not much one could do about it. He just wasn't as fancy as a hunter should be in front, and neither was he a big jumper prospect. He was a lovely little Quarter Horse with a poor style of jumping.

"Never mind," she said. *"I will teach him to be a dressage horse. We have Karl Mikolka in the barn, and with your help and Karl's help, I will train a dressage horse."* She had never done that before.

Little by little, with everyone's help, and everyone acting, this horse became a Fourth-Level dressage horse. He did it beautifully and he loved it. Jan also loved it, even though she was showing hunters at one end of the stick. She was training a Fourth-Level dressage horse by herself because he wasn't a hunter. I was so proud of her, and that horse found a wonderful home as a dressage horse and went on to please a lot of people. She recognized right away what a good horseman should recognize: the horse was not predestined to be a hunter; he was predestined to be a dressage horse. He was happy in his work, he loved it, and he did it well.

Part of the responsibility of someone who likes to train has got to be to recognize the tendency of a horse and to try to make him his personal best in a discipline that he loves. Sometimes, the made horses are so expensive that you cannot afford to buy the seven- or eight-year-old horse which has already become a good jumper, hunter, or dressage horse. So, you say, *"All right, I can spend the money for a three-year-old, and I will train that horse to be my next hunter."* What if he doesn't lend himself to that discipline? You cannot just discard him and throw him out. You should follow him in his direction and broaden your own ability to train a horse. You should put the horse in the place where he belongs and where he can be happy for the rest of his life.

Training a horse can produce great joy for the trainer, but it is not because of what the trainer receives from the horse. It is what the horse receives from the trainer that produces this feeling of complete satisfaction at the end of the job. You can recognize a horse which is happy in his job. When it was time to take off for the 2016 Rio Olympics, and Kevin Staut had already gone, and I gave his horse Reveur one last little exercise on the longe line, Reveur bucked and played. He had really come to the top of his game and he loved what he was doing. He had learned to do a pirouette and he could do middle trot from the halt. He learned all of this and it brightened his spirit, and he could buck like a young horse.

He went off to Rio and was part of the Gold Medal team. He did a wonderful job and supported his team. He was 17 years old. This was a horse at the top of his game due to the fact that the training was all centered around his personality. Everything was for that horse. If you train a horse that wins a gold medal or the Kentucky Derby or the Champion of the Hunt in the Washington International Horse Show, you have reason to be proud. But if you train a horse that can't even canter but can do a levade, and 10 kids learn to ride the levade on that horse, you can feel the same pride and pleasure in having brought a horse to his own personal best.

This is the way I look at training horses. In my lifetime, I've trained a lot of horses; I've trained them to do all sorts of things. But I don't care what I train them in or in which discipline. I care that they get to their personal best.

CHAPTER TWENTY-THREE
KEVIN'S NEW BEGINNING

Kevin's grandparents had built a lovely stable on the hill in Pennedepie years ago, with a view to Kevin's possible installation at home. The stable has a view of the ocean, which is close enough to reach on a horse. There is a wonderful ring with perfect footing, a U-shaped barn with a saddling area in the middle, an office and lounges in the corners, and a wash stall at the end of one of the wings. No permit could be acquired from the town for the construction of an indoor arena. Kevin was allowed to build a large walker instead. He built the walker but never installed the actual machine, so as to use the small building as a place to longe or ride in case of a real downpour. It worked very well to warm up a frisky horse as well, or to channel a spooky one before moving to the ring below.

After a time, a new group of stalls was built and the group of horses became larger. But it remains a small private place to train in bucolic conditions and the quiet ambiance that Kevin likes for the horses. I have been privileged to teach and ride the horses that come to prepare, and we have had some good young assistant riders who are learning the method while helping Kevin with the conditioning of his horses. Many of these young people are becoming professionals now and the progression is fun to watch. One of the first young riders I encouraged to come was Mathis Burnouf, the same young man that I had taken with me to Wellington one year. He had great success competing horses for Kevin and continues to ride in good classes on his own.

I later brought Hugo Paris to Kevin's attention. Hugo rode at the farm for quite some time before forming an association with his family in La

Manche. Later, Estelle Navet came to ride. Estelle is another favorite of mine, a good student, modest, and a good rider. I particularly like to train young riders as I know they are the future of the sport. If I train them well, and they are riding Kevin's horses, they are a big help to our team and are individually involved in the horses. All members of a team must feel involved in order for a team spirit to evolve. All members must feel their own progress in whatever part they play. The ambiance created by a team spirit makes the work fun and rewarding, and it is terribly important for the top rider in the group. If there is to be success at the highest level, as much energy as is devoted to the horses must be devoted to the creation of the ambiance. We are more than lucky in our team spirit; we are dedicated to it.

New horses arrived from several sources to the stable in Pennedepie. One of my favorite mares, Tolede, proved to be a real team player. I laughed when I first rode her because as I looked down when I settled into the saddle, I realized that I was riding a huge Shetland pony. Tolede is short in the neck and shoulder, but with a huge engine in the back. What is visible to the rider is not an indication of what she can do. Her character is generous, steady, and honest. She is easy to train and the important work to improve her is easy to do. She needs to stretch her neck and separate her shoulders in order to become looser in the front. She likes to do this, and I could teach all the kids how to do the same. She has been a household staple ever since she arrived. William and Caroline Benguigui are great owners and they loved their mare. They also sent a young horse, Emir, that I loved to ride but was a puzzle. Emir jumped too low. He was rarely clear but always jumped.

Kevin is a rider who rarely gives up. Emir presented a challenge and it seemed impossible to find a solution. Finally, as a drastic idea, Kevin removed his shoes. I have never been a complete fan of this new fad, but one needs to be open-minded. With Emir, the difference was immediate and dramatic. He began to move his shoulder, jump higher, and stay longer in the air. Within three months, he was jumping the bigger classes and placing regularly! He was happy to land without the constriction of shoes. As I love this horse, his new comfort was a joy to me. One learns and relearns that the horse will let you know what he needs, if you only keep an open mind and try things. No two horses are alike.

Visconti presented another challenge entirely. She has incredible scope, a huge stride, a cool mind, and a slow front end. To add to this, she had the balance of a wheelbarrow. Any rider reading that description will see that there would be a problem with the tall verticals. There are two solutions to riding this type of horse. One is to stay as far away from the jump as possible at the takeoff to give the horse enough time to get his front legs up. Our mare was obedient, and Kevin is accurate to a fault. This was the method he decided to use. I can remember, at Vilamoura in Portugal, the day Kevin said to me, "It's impossible to find the room in front of every jump at this height to be clear." The mare was jumping the 1.45m and 1.50m.

We discussed the second solution to this type of horse, which is to change the balance of the canter with which one approaches the jump. This involves dressage and certain movements at the canter which educate and strengthen the horse. Our mare was obedient. Kevin can do anything he decides to try. Within a few weeks, the mare had learned the job in another way. Within a few days, Kevin felt a difference and a possibility of jumping clear. One must be present at all times, as the mare is somewhat rider-dependent. She likes this ride. It was a huge thrill when she was double clear in the 1.60m Nations Cup in Rome, to be on the winning team after a very short time with this new method. Knowing her whole story made it even more of a pleasure. Her owner, who lives for her mare, is Françoise Sanguinetti, and her pleasure was a reward in itself.

Bruno Roquet sent us a wonderful mare, Iliade, that he liked a lot. At the time she arrived, her potential was difficult to determine but her intelligence, courage, and respect made everyone hope that her scope would allow her to do the high levels. The work to improve this mare was not complicated for the rider with simple lateral and suppling movements. But the mare found the new work a challenge. She is a trier, so it only took patience. She loosened up into a top competitor, and the whole team was able to enjoy the progress of a good mare once again. Bruno was absolutely right in his instinct about the mare!

Good horses continued to arrive, each one to be diagnosed and to be put in the right program. Jamesbond, Dialou, Cheppetta; no one horse like another, but Kevin rode them all. For me, the hardest horse to analyze was

Viking. I was never allowed to ride or longe Viking due to his habit of trying every new rider. He is a contortionist. He can buck, rear, and spin, and do combinations of all of these. He is also an Olympic quality jumper that finds 1.60m jumps easy. He usually goes to work after the first two jumps, but there is no guarantee. Kevin is always alert to Viking's mood. His expression is hard to read and there is no warning about what he is considering. When I cannot read the mind of a horse, it is hard to devise a plan. Some of the best horses have the most character. Viking is independent and a little hard-hearted so Kevin has reached a compromise with him that took some time. It is a great credit to Kevin's adaptive skills that Viking has become one of his best horses and a solid representative of France.

When I went to ride at Reiner Klimke's stable in Münster, Germany, he told me that he did not teach, but that I could watch. Later, he let me learn from riding all of his horses and also those of Ruth. Young riders at Kevin's learn the same way. They watch and set fences. They are able to ride his horses between shows. They are allowed to jump on the given horse under his supervision or mine, and sometimes allowed to show.

I can remember one day I was schooling Hugo Paris, who was allowed to jump Vendôme, a nine-year-old at the time. Vendôme was extremely obedient and reflected years of correct riding by Delphine Perez and then Kevin. Hugo jumped around the course after having warmed up over a few small jumps. The expression on his face told how much he had learned by riding a well-schooled horse. He was impressed and he was very happy. This ride, given to Hugo by Kevin, was to show Hugo the way to form his own horses in the future. A rider learns more from a horse with a trainer beside him than he learns from the trainer alone. The feeling is more important than the word. Taking lessons on very well-schooled horses is the fastest way to learn.

Vendôme was not alone in his ability to form riders at Kevin's stable. Qurack de Falaise was at the end of his career when I came, and I used him a lot to teach flying changes every four and every three strides, and other movements in dressage. He had such a lovely character, I could teach him any movement even though he had never been a dressage horse. He would repeat that for anyone. He has a special place in my heart where he is a winner.

Dialou, a bay mare of six years when she arrived, was ridden at the beginning by Estelle. Kevin allowed us to get the mare ready for some classes for Estelle to compete. The mare was afraid of others in the schooling area, or in the ring at home, and could spin pretty quickly. She was a great jumper and very careful. She was so careful at the beginning that one day she stopped at a rather tall vertical at home, rather than jump from a less-than-perfect distance and risk touching the jump. I learned a lot and so did Estelle when she tried a different approach to the same jump. The mare jumped, but with a huge exaggeration of her technique.

I stopped Estelle; we gave a carrot and a short break to the mare. We knew we had a good one! I never punish a careful horse for a stop in this situation. Dialou was not a stopper. She was a green, careful six-year-old. The fact that she improved her technique to cope with difficulty showed her physical potential and her intelligence. Punishment would have been the wrong approach.

Estelle and I had a problem in that Kevin was riding in the ring with us, and he saw what a good mare she was. We knew she was destined for his group. We laughed about that a lot. Indeed, after a few months of careful showing, Kevin began to ride the mare and she was the trier we all saw on that day. I love mares, actually prefer mares, because they are transparent. One can easily follow their reasoning and make quick and logical adjustments to the program. Adjusting a program is never ceding the point. It is the intelligent way to get to the destination with the minimum of stress and struggle. Within two years, this wonderful mare was placing in the smaller Grand Prix of 1.50m, and is now jumping the bigger classes with great self-confidence.

Kevin gave Estelle a nice horse, Bon Jovi in Live, to ride in the bigger classes. He could be competitive in the speed phase. She was able to win some prizes and improve her confidence in that phase due to the horse. We were sorry to see Estelle leave us and go back to school.

While Mathis was riding for Kevin, he was given a young stallion to ride and show, CCStud's Fidelity. This horse had one weakness which taught Mathis a lot. He became disunited around every turn in both directions. This is not difficult to correct if one knows to use the outside rein. Instead of repeating, "Use your outside rein to support the canter around the turns," it was easy to give Mathis this horse who made it very clear. Mathis loves to win and he got the message! He went off to Valkensvaard with the horse to show and won a prize in every class. The young stallion returned to Sweden to do both competition and to stand at stud. We had a series of young assistant riders who were fun to train at the same time that the main concern was Kevin's top group of horses and the competition at the extreme levels.

After Rio and the team gold medal for France, with the group of horses being older, it was time to concentrate on accumulating and developing new candidates. The Vivaldi Syndicate made the acquisition of Viking and Cheppetta possible, both being Olympic hopefuls. New owners arrived with all types of nice horses to the stable in Pennedepie. Jean-Louis Roudaut brought his horse Blackonda over in the truck for Kevin to school, and then followed the horse to every show. This was a great help to the whole group of horses. A time of reconstruction had arrived, and while these horses were learning the method, Kevin lost his place in the top 10 world classification. No one lost hope and the morale was high at the stable as we could all see that there was about to be a big reawakening. When the new group began to emerge, Kevin moved up to position 10 right away, and we waited for more with assurance.

♊

RIDING LESSON

It is one of the most important responsibilities of the rider and trainer of every horse to recognize his limit. This limit may change over time as the horse becomes older, stronger, more educated, more confident, or, in the case of a horse of 10 or more years, older, weaker, stiffer, and less agile. The limit of any horse is a moving target.

The limit must be respected. A speed limit on the highway is enforced by the law. The performance limit of a horse is enforced by the consequence of going too far, or not far enough. The list of consequences is long. Many are not easy to fix.

The Consequences of Going Too Far:

1. The horse can lose confidence in his rider. This can usually be fixed by changing the rider for one with a better instinct.

2. The horse can lose confidence in himself. This is much harder to overcome, and only time and positive experience will fix the loss.

3. The horse can resort to a poor or dangerous technique in order to do what is asked. In fact, one of the important signs of asking too much is the loss of good technique. It is said by the old masters that a horse who repeats a bad technique three times will then be habitual in the error for his lifetime. This was said in the late 1600s pertaining to the flying change, but it is true today and it pertains to jumping.

4. The horse can be injured physically. Even if the horse does not fall or stumble, it is possible to twist or strain a muscle, ligament, or tendon

RECOGNIZING THE LIMIT

through severe effort. Time, and a veterinarian with patience, will probably fix the issue but there is no returning to the original state of the horse.

5. The horse can learn defense tactics which become behavioral problems. Once the horse is forced to protect himself, his defense will be according to the danger posed. Controlling the defense without eliminating the perceived danger will only produce a different and stronger defense. All learned defenses remain embedded in the horse's memory. This, of all, is the most serious of consequences. A real professional must take over from a very low level to reprogram this type of horse.

The Consequences of Not Going Far Enough:

There is another limit to respect, which is rarely discussed: the limit which is too low regarding the challenge posed to a horse in his daily work. This, too, is a moving target.

1. The younger horse must be challenged intellectually such that his education is more important than his physical condition and degree of fitness. If the proportion is wrong, an extremely fit, uneducated young horse becomes hard to control and requires a very physical and strong rider. This is dangerous for the joints of the horse and also for the possibility of awakening the defense mechanisms already discussed.

The proportion of intellectual work versus physical conditioning is correct when the horse begins the day with the idea of learning and working with the rider, not against the rider. Intellectual work with a young horse is tricky because it must be within his limit to understand. If the horse does not understand and find the solution within three or four minutes, the demand is beyond the intellectual limit of the horse or badly presented.

2. Boredom is the consequence of riding below the level of the horse. Repetition is not education. Education requires new material. A rider or trainer of a young horse must possess a huge source of ideas to present to the horse, all of which are within the limit of a four-year-old, both physically and mentally. Repetition is part of conditioning. To develop a certain strength, one repeats an effort. Repetition is boring. It is useful in its place, but as a method of training, with no intellectual stimulation, there are consequences to this. Just as a smart student in a slow class in his school starts to daydream, write notes, or create mischief, a young horse trained by repetition will start to leave the classroom.

Signs the Level Is Too High:

- Poor quality of movement or posture, such as an impure canter, hind legs apart at the trot, neck too short, nose behind the vertical, or the horse moving in a crooked way.

- Jumping in a poor technique, such as too quickly, not judging the height of the jump, twisting or displacing the shoulders left or right to avoid hitting the jump, trajectory not well designed, or changes of speed or the lead within the last strides.

- A lack of confidence, calmness, and concentration. Anxiety, hysteria, and inattentiveness indicate a horse beyond his level.

- Using defense methods to try to eliminate the danger, such as stopping, running away, running sideways, going towards the exit, and bucking, always indicates a horse beyond his limit.

Signs the Level Is Too Low:

- Boredom, lack of spark, inertia, dull eye, and lack of brilliance are usually seen in horses below their level.

- Jumping too low, trajectories too short, jumping too flat, and thinking too slowly are all results of being too far away from the potential of the horse.

The level of the horse must be accurately analyzed. Working at a level too high is as bad as working at a level that is too low.

The Older Horse

The work of an older horse is what determines the length of his career. He must be kept supple, so that becomes the priority in his conditioning. He must also learn something intellectually every week. If he learns nothing, he becomes stale, old, and slow-thinking. The rider of an old horse must possess a huge source of new ideas to present to an older horse which are within his reach physically and stimulate him mentally. Repetition is not new education. A rider must know more than the horse he rides. A trainer always knows more than the horses he trains.

Recapitulation

In general, the younger riders need to be aware of the higher limit of their horse and to see the signs that indicate they are too close to it. Repeating the work at a level too high for the horse will never ensure that he attains the level. It is far more likely that he will suffer the consequences listed above. In general, older riders need to be aware of the consequences of riding at a level too low for their horse. Repetition of work at a low level will not preserve the horse, but in fact will accelerate the aging process.

One must recognize the limit of the horse.

CHAPTER TWENTY-FOUR
THE SPORT OF KINGS AND OTHER ADVENTURES

My neighbors in Bourgeauville, Amelie and Robert Ehrnrooth, were engaged in the breeding of Thoroughbreds to be sold at the world-renowned Deauville Yearling Sales. Their wonderful Haras de Bourgeauville, with its lovely small château and acres of pastures, was heaven for the small but carefully selected group of broodmares. Amelie and Robert spent half their time in their native Finland and the other half in Bourgeauville. Their home was my second home, and I learned a lot about breeding racehorses, the various sales around the world, and what to do when the yearling is not sold.

Amelie's son, Philip Lybec, who runs Haras de Bourgeauville for his parents, married an expert in the pre-training of racehorses. Diane Lybec is the owner and director of Ecuries Diane, which can have as many as 100 horses in pre-training. Yearlings usually go into pre-training soon after the yearling sales in order to run or to prepare for the breeze-up sales in the spring. Some of the horses bred by Haras de Bourgeauville go into pre-training and then are sent to a trainer to race. Such a mare was Sarah Lynx.

Racehorses are horses, simply said. They may be bred to run but many top show jumpers and three-day eventers have been found in the Thoroughbred world. Sarah Lynx, by Montjeu, was purchased by Amelie as a very young mare to race and then be a broodmare. She did not want the job. She would not work in the morning and the riders had a hard time staying on when she balked. She did not want to come out of the starting box. She had not found the joy of running and was even crabby in the box. Her very good trainer sent her back to the Haras for a break. It was just at the time that a Finnish girl, Laura Vaska, who loved riding, came to visit Amelie and Robert.

We took the mare out into a field of cows. She did not like cows so it was easy to ride her around them and let her boss them a bit at first. She flattened her ears like a cutting horse! Then we took the mare away from the cows and let her trot back into the herd. Then we took her further and she cantered back. Pretty soon, we could trot away and canter back. Finally, Laura took the mare out to the fence line of the field, started to canter, and then sent her into a gallop. The mare flew! She also grew at least a hand when she went into a speed I had never seen in my life. Laura was impressed and thrilled by the feeling. When Laura pulled her up, she had forgotten the cows. I went into the château to get my friends, Amelie and Robert, and they came to watch. She did it again. She had changed her mind about galloping once she went at that speed.

The trainer was called and the mare went back to the track, keeping the secret of her work with cows. The trainer said that the vacation had done her a world of good, and he entered her in the One Million Dollar Race at Woodbine in Canada. Laura was to accompany the mare on the trip. She was the only filly in the race and the only horse running with no Lasix. The use of Lasix, a blood thinner, has now been restricted in many countries but has always been against the principles of Haras de Bourgeauville. She got the cover picture in *The Blood Horse* magazine when she won the race handily.

Laura left to take her place in the Darley Program, for three years of extensive study involving the Thoroughbred industry. She gained her trainer's license in France. She is now producing her own winners.

Racehorses are horses, simply said. The same psychological approach works on all horses. They have to find the joy in their job. When they do, they are winners. Sometimes more is what works. Sometimes less is what works.

During this time, I was also coaching other riders. Amy Graham, who was based in Normandy, rode for her native Australia. She was asked to do the two Nations Cups as a qualifier for the 2020 Tokyo Olympics. We spent a long time preparing her wonderful mare, Coleraine. This brave and scopey mare was half owned by Amy's family and half by her breeder,

Philippe Jadot Bergeries. We went to Florida to do the Nations Cups at Wellington and Amy rode at her best. For the second and most important of the Nations Cups, she was very sick and had not been able to ride for days. How she pulled herself into the saddle to help her team to the third place on that podium was an example of team spirit. Australians are hardy folk.

While in Spain for the Sunshine Tour, I met Italian Luca Moneta, who asked me if we could train together. Luca is a unique horseman who has his own method of training horses in liberty and with no bridle. He has ridden for Italy at the very highest level in his own system. Dressage was far from his idea of training, but he was willing to try it. He immediately agreed that this type of training can be done without all the domination of the horse that one occasionally sees. We have worked together most enjoyably ever since, always hunting for the right path for every horse. He juggles a life filled with students and clinics with a big show schedule. It's hard to train at shows so we try to organize time out for training at his stable near Milan. This is a magical place for horses and a perfect place to train. Italian wine and cheese is equal to the French!

When I met Luca, I also met Guy Jonqueres d'Oriola. We began to work, all three of us, at shows and at training sessions, in an attempt to get to the bigger classes and to improve the big group of nice horses that they rode. They each have two parts to their life with horses. Luca rides competitively very well, but he is equally engaged in teaching his method of groundwork and riding with no bridle to those interested in understanding how a horse thinks. The biggest challenge for the trainer is to add more information without interfering with Luca's existing career.

I joke with Guy about him having Sport One and Sport Two. His Sport One is the sport of riding and competing at the high level. He is serious and competent with the method he has learned, and competes several horses at this level, having done the top category French Championship and many Grand Prix successfully. Guy enjoys method. Having the most information possible about the course to be ridden or the horse to be trained makes Guy secure and positive in his approach. Guy, like Karl Mikolka and me, is a taught rider. Horses take great confidence from this no-surprises approach. The mistakes are quickly forgotten and the horse remains positive. Guy does a remarkable job using a base of method.

Sport Two for Guy is the sport of selling nice horses to clients from all around the world. His spare time is filled with finding these horses and traveling with clients. It is a real organization to do both, with me pushing for Sport One. Sometimes, I push to keep the horses for Guy that he would like to sell. Guy likes horses and they like him. It usually takes no more than a few rides for horses to realize that he is kind. He can ride almost any type of horse, but he needs to ride the horse for a week before the bond is made. I have learned to wait.

Life with students of this dedication and love of horses at the same time is a great pleasure to me. I am competitive. I am very protective of my competition horses. They are hard to find and they take enormous support. I take no joy in competing at a level beyond my horses. I take no joy in competing an unhappy or unsound horse. My riders feel the same, and we make a good team.

I like teaching and I like training horses at any level. Everything starts somewhere. Improvement is possible at any level. In a classical training method, the method is as important as the level of success. One can apply, again and again, the same method on other horses and expect the same result. The logic of the classical teachings is inescapable. There are no two horses which are exactly alike, although they usually fall into a category. Being trained in several classical methods allows a rider to find the easiest way to train more horses. Exactly in the same way that speaking several languages enables communication with more people, employing the method that suits a given horse makes life easier.

Everyone has their own favorite ride or method. But the horse is always the deciding factor. A rider or a trainer cannot be locked into a way of riding that is not palatable to a given horse. My own preference in training is the Weyrother system, which is the one taught at the Spanish Riding School. I am equally happy to ride in the Caprilli method, also known as the American Hunter method. I am happy when my horse understands me and is open to communication. I am unhappy when my horse is closed, stuck, and non-communicative.

My father could only speak English. When I was about 13, he took the family on a tour of Europe one summer. In Germany, he asked for directions at a crossroads in English. When he was not understood, he asked again but louder! He tried a third time with greater volume! Finally, we went on to find our way, unaided by the poor countryman whose ears were ringing.

So many riders make the same error in turning up the volume of their training when it is not understood, instead of finding the right language, or system, for the horse involved. This never works and creates a frustrated and defensive horse for someone to retrain—a job I love.

A principle that I like to teach is that there is never a need to use force in training a horse. There is a huge need to use education. It is impossible to have the education required without going to school. Most schools only teach one method. One method is insufficient to be a trainer unless horses are selected by their preference for that method. Some people select horses in this way, saying, "He is my ride." It is much better to be able to adjust to the horse, and in doing so, ride using the language understood. This is the spirit of horsemanship.

When I train most older experienced riders, the challenge is to convince them to try other ways than their own to do things that are not working. Kevin is unusual in that he loves to find new ways and to learn new techniques. Most riders enjoying success are nervous to change anything. In this way, they become blocked and stagnated in their riding. It takes courage to experiment. There is no universal system for all horses. Education must take preference over instinct in many areas.

I like to train riders who have not yet become convinced of one single approach. Flexibility is important in a rider, but flexibility between acceptable classical methods is preferable to the invention of unusual unique bits, auxiliary reins, and bizarre gymnastics. Everything one needs has been included in the classical methods. One has only to open a book, or find a teacher.

One of the beauties of using classical riding to solve problems is that the side effects of the solution are always beneficial. For example, a horse with a high head carriage can be easily controlled with draw reins. The side effects are very bad: strong under neck, shortened stride in the hind leg, and restricted shoulder over the jump. The same horse, corrected by the use of shoulder-in, is a different story! The hind leg becomes stronger and more engaged, the outside shoulder becomes freer and looser, and the top line becomes rounder and stronger at the same time that the horse drops his head. For every challenge in the education of a horse, there is a solution in one of the classical methods of training.

A knowledgeable man once told me that a trainer will resort to force when he reaches the limit of his education. When the horse refuses to get onto the truck, the trainer begins to try everything he knows to coerce the horse to load. When after everything that he knows to do fails, he resorts to force. One can judge the education of a trainer by the time it takes for him to resort to force.

How often do I think, longingly, about a horse owned years ago—given the new information accumulated during the years passed since then, how much I would like a second chance. Many riders have had this sentiment. The solution to most challenges is found in education. It is rarely found in strength, force, or gadgets.

If there is anything that I have learned in my life with horses, it is that one never knows enough. This is a lifelong pursuit of information. The horse presents a never-ending kaleidoscope of personality quirks and individual reactions to his education process. It is this fascinating challenge that provides the opportunity for growth. Every difficulty must be regarded in this light. A teacher's most important influence on his students is to produce this outlook on the handling of horses. It would be my great pride to think that I could have so inspired some of my own students. It would be an even greater pride to know that some of those so influenced would influence others to come later.

EPILOGUE

The end should be the beginning. Beginnings are born with challenges, motivations, new ideas, and contrasts. It is what I hope to produce in my teaching and in the methods I have used to try to make my horses the best that they can be.

The horse is always the priority in the triangle of Rider-Trainer-Horse. It is the responsibility of the trainer to ensure this priority. The enormous pressure of winning, of making money, of sales commissions, and of ego, all laid on the back of the horse, must be identified and set aside. The horse can only carry a rider.

The relationship between a rider and his horse is first made possible by the trainer, who selects the best method of approach. The character of the horse, and not the character of the rider or trainer, must determine the approach. Time is well saved by the right choice at the beginning. A confident horse is easy to train. The rider of a calm and comfortable horse learns quickly in the absence of fear. Frustration is always to be avoided and can be eliminated through education and a correct choice of techniques from the very start.

There are two stages in teaching. In the beginning, the teacher must inspire the student. All energy is coming from the teacher to the student. Information and directives are energy, as well as praise, correction, and a certain amount of theatrics. Well done, this first stage of teaching will lead to the second stage.

In the second stage, the student inspires the teacher. This, then, is the reward of teaching. The student is then likely to end up as a teacher, or at least a very good rider. The future of our sport and our outlook regarding the horse who permits this life depends on today's teachers. Reiner Klimke told me that his greatest joy was in producing a horse to the level of Grand Prix without losing the horse's joyful spirit. The greatest joy of a teacher is similar, in that the student exemplifies the spirit of the trainer as he reaches the highest levels.

My book is meant to explain these riches and to motivate those who follow them to find them as well as I have.

RECOMMENDED READING

A partial list of reading material is given here, as promised, to start the rider who is new to learning by reading. These books are classic, correct, and basic. They have also been written in a way as to be extremely palatable.

At the end of this list, I will enclose some of the authors that are, if not less palatable to the novice reader, even more profound in the knowledge of the art of riding.

Start with these, and once inspired, go further:

De Nemethy, Bertalan. *The De Nemethy Method.* (1988) Doubleday.

Emerson, Denny. *How Good Riders Get Good.* (2019) Trafalgar Square Books.

General Decarpentry. *Academic Equitation.* (2001) Trafalgar Square Books.

Karl, Philippe. *Twisted Truths of Modern Dressage.* (2008) Cadmos Publishing.

Klimke, Reiner, and Klimke, Ingrid. *Basic Training of the Young Horse.* (2015) Trafalgar Square Books.

Littauer, Vladimir. *Common Sense Horsemanship.* (1974) Arco.

Morris, George. *Hunter Seat Equitation.* (1990) Doubleday.

Müseler, Wilhelm. *Riding Logic.* (2021) Trafalgar Square Books.

Ostergaard, Gunnar. *Life as a Dressage Trainer in Three Countries.* (2024) Four In Hand Press.

Podhajsky, Alois. *The Riding Teacher.* (1993) Trafalgar Square Books.

Wright, Gordon. *Learning to Ride, Hunt and Show.* (1950) Sky Horse Publishing.

Once the appetite is whetted, one can try these manuals intended as reference books, but which supply all the answers to the individual problem. This list of authors is incomplete, but exemplary:

Baucher, François. *New Method of Horsemanship.* (1800) Albert Cogswell. Available here: *https://archive.org/details/newmethodofhorse00bauc/page/n7/mode/2up*

Lt. Col. A. L. D'Enrody. *Give Your Horse a Chance.* (2012) Trafalgar Square Books.

Seunig, Waldemar. *Horsemanship: A Comprehensive Book on Training the Horse and its Rider.* (1956) J. A. Allen & Co.

Steinbrecht, Gustav. *Gymnasium of the Horse* (1994). Xenophon Press.

Be well equipped; be well read.

ACKNOWLEDGMENTS

I'd like to thank all my many friends and students who made it easy to fill these pages. I would also like to thank all my teachers who taught me to think like a horse. Specifically, I'd like to thank my best friend and technical advisor, emotional support expert, and fellow adventurer, Sandra Ball Markus. I would also like to thank Kevin Messaoudi, who keeps my dog, Roberto, when I travel so as to give me peace of mind.

♊

ABOUT THE AUTHOR

Julie Ulrich learned riding and horsemanship from such esteemed horsemen as former Chief Rider at the Spanish Riding School Karl Mikolka, German Olympian Reiner Klimke, and Show Jumping Hall of Fame Inductee Frances Rowe. She successfully competed in multiple disciplines throughout her life, including hunters, dressage, and show jumping. Her specialty has always been show jumping, and it is in this discipline that she trains riders and horses. Ulrich was brought up in Minnesota and later developed a huge training facility, Friars Gate Farm, with her husband Richard, in Pembroke, Massachusetts. She later moved a smaller version of Friars Gate Farm to Middleburg, Virginia, closer to fox hunting country—an activity she loves. Ulrich eventually emigrated to Normandy, France, where she currently lives. Throughout her life, Ulrich has shared her knowledge with students, and she still regularly teaches and trains in the United States and Europe.

♊